~~START~~ STARTUP YOUR CAREER

THINK BIG, START EARLY, SCALE YOUR CAREER FAST

Raghav

ISBN 979-8-89322-665-2

This book is a tribute to the amazing women who have been the bedrock of my existence and career. Your endless love, support, and encouragement have been my greatest blessings. Your guidance has not only shaped me personally but has also been instrumental in my professional journey. I am eternally thankful for every moment shared, every lesson learned, and every challenge overcome with you by my side.

Table of Contents

Introduction

In June 2022, I stepped onto a plane bound for Thailand. It was my third visit to the country, but this time I was on an extended sabbatical, a pause I had earned after intense years as the Director of Business at a Series A startup. There, I had taken a nascent pharmaceutical business and nurtured it into something formidable, achieving an 80-fold growth without any prior background in the field. This success was a beacon, urging me to reevaluate what I was capable of and nudging me towards a calling in entrepreneurship that had whispered to me since I was eight years old.

Back then, I had started my first venture: breeding and selling fancy fish to my neighbors. It was more than a childhood pastime; it was a venture that generated thousands monthly, a testament to the entrepreneurial spirit that has always pulsed within me. Over the years, as I traveled to 19 countries, each journey added layers to my understanding of business, culture, and self. Yet, it was my recent trip to Thailand that became a definitive pivot, a moment that crystallized my decision to fully embrace entrepreneurship.

I cannot speak of this shift without acknowledging my mentor, Krishnan, whose guidance was both a map and a compass in my journey. Today, I stand at a different vantage point, marking a year as the Co-founder of a bootstrapped SAAS startup. It's a role that I stepped into with a blend of anticipation and confidence, carrying with me the lessons from my past and the promise of the future.

Throughout my journey, I've often found myself pondering the complex relationship between hard work and success. It's a riddle that has followed me from the eager days of my fresh graduation to the reflective evenings as a self-made CXO. Why do some toil endlessly and barely move the needle, while others, seemingly touched by an invisible hand, ascend swiftly up the ladder of success? This question isn't just philosophical musing; it's a personal inquiry into the nature of achievement and the elusive recipe for prosperity.

My own path has been a testament to the unpredictability of this equation. I dove into the professional world right after college, carrying a blend of naivety and determination. Over the years, my trajectory from a novice graduate to an entrepreneur with a multimillion-dollar startup has been both astonishing and illuminating. With Kaay Innovation's support, We bootstrapped our company to a 2.5 million revenue in a mere eight months. Yet, this wasn't a straightforward journey of linear progress. It was a winding path marked by introspection, strategic pivots, and a relentless pursuit of something beyond the conventional markers of success.

In the last five years, as I've interacted with thousands and mentored hundreds, I've observed the myriad ways people approach their careers and aspirations. I've seen the fire of ambition in the eyes of many, a desire so intense yet often misdirected or extinguished by unforeseen challenges. My experiences led me to a profound realization: while I can't decode the entire mystery of success, I can contribute a chapter to the narrative. This realization was the seed that grew into 'Startup Your Career.'

'Startup Your Career' is the crystallization of my journey, my insights, and my desire to light the path for others. It's a space where individuals can come to learn and transform. Here, the ethos is about scaling your careers, perspectives, ambitions, and the very sense of self. It's about nurturing that 'plus one' - the additional step, the extra mile, the next leap - that distinguishes the extraordinary from the ordinary.

As I pen this book, I stand at the threshold of yet another personal transformation. This endeavor extends beyond merely writing a text, it's about crafting the subsequent chapter of my life. The process embodies self-reinvention, a profound and occasionally intimidating exploration of my inner self. It involves confronting the ego, expanding the limits of comfort, and focusing on a horizon of unparalleled excellence. This journey represents my dedication to discovering the finest version of myself, a pursuit aimed at deep and lasting fulfillment.

01

Elevate Your Aim

The room was drenched in heavy silence, punctuated only by the rhythmic ticking of the chess clock. On one side of the board sat Grandmaster Ivanov, a seasoned player who had faced countless adversaries in his storied career. But today's match was different. It was a contest against not just another player but against his own future.

The predicament Ivanov found himself in was mirrored in the position of his pieces. He had a choice to make: to go for a daring sacrifice that could lead to a brilliant victory or play it safe, solidifying his position and waiting for a more opportune moment. This decision wasn't just about this game, it was symbolic of the choices we make in our professional lives.

Do we play it safe, maintaining the status quo and slowly progressing? Or do we take calculated risks, setting audacious goals, even if they come with the possibility of failure? Ivanov's fingers hovered over his knight. The weight of the decision bore down on him.

In his mind, the chessboard transformed. The pieces were no longer just wood and ivory but represented various facets of his career. The pawns were his daily tasks and responsibilities. The rooks and knights represented his skills and strategies, while the queen symbolized his ultimate career goals.

The next move would determine not just the outcome of the game, but also his approach to challenges, opportunities, and growth. As he moved his knight to a forward square, exposing it but opening up possibilities, it became clear. This wasn't a mere game of chess. It was a testament to the power of anticipation, of setting goals, and the profound consequences they bear in our professional trajectories.

Years later, reflecting on his illustrious career, Ivanov would often recall that match. Not because of its result, but because of the lesson it engraved in him. In the intricate aspects of professional interactions, it's not always about the immediate move. It's about seeing the endgame, setting the stage for what lies ahead, and most importantly, understanding the profoundness of each choice we make on our journey to career ascension.

Redefining Goals

The professional world often frames goals as static endpoints, markers we unrelentingly chase. But to view them merely as final destinations is to miss out on the intricate narratives that unfold along the way.

Ponder this: the two-pronged nature of professional growth. On one hand, there's vertical growth – the climb up the corporate ladder, the quest for promotions, and the allure of higher titles. On the other, there's horizontal growth – a venture into diverse skill sets, a broadening of one's professional network, and a thirst to gather varied experiences. What if our goals were attuned to both these aspects, not just guiding us to a specific pinnacle but also charting the vast terrains awaiting exploration?

In this reimagined paradigm, goals aren't just finish lines. They're dynamic, evolving signposts. They guide our ascent upwards, while also ensuring our strides span outward, enriching us in every dimension.

Drawing parallels with our chess analogy, this calls for a viewpoint beyond mere titles or milestones. It's about forging a trajectory where our ambitions recalibrate, similar to how a grandmaster remains fluid, anticipating and counteracting each move. The takeaway? Visualize professional goals as dual-level entities – catalysts for both elevation and expansion. The game isn't just about reaching the king, it's about mastering the board.

In the initial months of my role as a sales manager at Colgate, a realization struck me, similar to the chess pieces suddenly gaining sharper focus. Who exactly were my teammates? The vast network of individuals, each contributing to the intricate workings of corporate operations, remained anonymous to me.

Being an introvert, I often found comfort in the shadows. Yet, my inclination wasn't rooted in a disdain for interactions. It was confidence, or the lack of it, that held me back. A pivotal decision awaited me.

Taking a deep breath, I reached out. From fresh recruits to seasoned veterans boasting a quarter-century of experience, I connected with colleagues, regardless of their tenure or location. My inquiry was simple but loaded with intent. The responses I received were enlightening.

While many prided themselves on ticking off tasks and earning commendations, a revelation stood out. One individual, despite their relatively short stint, was scaling the professional ladder at an accelerated pace. So, what was their secret? They understood the Goal+1 method and resonated with the ethos of their team. They listened, deciphered, and most importantly, acted in alignment with the company's broader vision.

It was a profound moment of clarity for me. More often than not, our superiors possess a bird's eye view of operations. They don't seek mere performers, they value contributors. While achievements might fetch incentives, it's the enhancement of the organizational mission that truly paves the way for ascension.

It wasn't just about setting personal objectives. It was about aligning them with the broader company goals and then going that extra mile – the "+1" in my Goal+1 method.

Grounded in Theory: Decoding the Compass of Aspirations

Have you ever felt lost amidst a myriad of tasks, wondering which direction to take? Locke and Latham, two visionary psychologists, presented a simple yet transformative idea: set clear and challenging goals. Instead of chasing vague aspirations, focus on the specifics. Imagine wanting to visit Europe but not knowing which country. Specificity, like deciding on Paris over just 'Europe', makes all the difference. It's not about a vague destination but a precise, desired spot. And remember, feedback is your travel guide, helping you adjust your journey.

New ideas can be exciting, but without a structured approach, where do you start? Enter the SMART criteria. SMART, an acronym for Specific, Measurable, Achievable, Relevant, and Time-bound ensures that your objectives are well-defined and attainable within a certain timeframe. It's your instruction manual, ensuring your ambitions have both wings and a flight path. Be like Bezos, not just dreaming of an online empire, but starting step by step, with books as the foundation.

These are not just theories, but actionable strategies that have stood the test of time in shaping careers. But here's a personal touch: my "Sand Clock Code." Inspired by the precision of an hourglass, it's a fusion of various principles to help you carve out a unique, efficient, and fruitful career path. Think of it as a crafted blend of traditional wisdom and modern insights, ensuring that as time slips, your aspirations remain firm and achievable.

The Sand Clock Code: Engineering Your Ascent

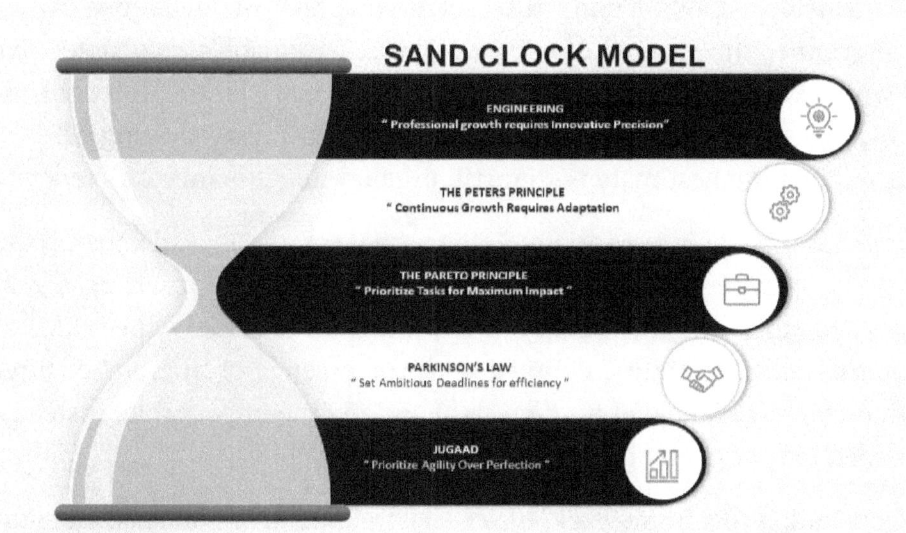

Engineering: At the heart of engineering lies not just the diploma that one might possess, but an innate ability to craft and create with precision and innovation. Let's delve into a more grounded analogy: Imagine an array of colorful Lego blocks. An engineer isn't just someone who can stack them up. It's the person who discerns the best approach to constructing them, be it for a towering castle or a resilient bridge for toy cars. The world of professional growth demands this very 'engineering' acumen, where goals are not merely met but crafted for excellence.

The Peters Principle: A revelation hit me when I first unearthed the layers of the Peters Principle. It eloquently posits, "What gets you here won't get you there." The competencies that elevated you to your current position might not suffice for the next leap. This realization is vital—by identifying and transcending our limitations, we can re-engineer our skillset for the subsequent stages of our journey.

Pareto's Principle: At its core, the Pareto Principle champions efficiency. It's about channeling your efforts into the 20% of tasks that yield 80% of the results. In my professional realm, this became the cornerstone of my productivity: discerning where my primary contributions lay and then pouring energy into those avenues.

Parkinson's Law: Time, the silent dictator of deadlines, often determines the success of our endeavors. Parkinson's Law states that "work expands to fill the time available for its completion." Recognizing this, my mantra became to set ambitious deadlines—shaving off 20% from my initial estimates—to instill urgency and enhance efficiency.

Jugaad: The quintessentially Indian concept of 'Jugaad' champions agility over perfection. It's about swift execution, improvising on the go, and embracing the beauty of imperfection to achieve the end goal. Speed and adaptability, coupled with the essence of 'Jugaad,' ensured that I wasn't entangled in the web of seeking the impeccable. Instead, I aimed for pragmatic perfection.

Concluding this framework, it's crucial to underscore one last element: personal branding. Ensure your contributions and capabilities are known not just to your immediate team but radiate outward. Seek acknowledgment from peers, superiors, and notably, skip-level managers. They're often the silent gatekeepers, holding the key to your next big leap.

Following the tailored structure of the Sand Clock Code, one might ask: "How do we set the trajectory for our dreams to take flight?" We often find ourselves enveloped in the allure of grand visions, but to truly soar, these dreams demand direction.

From Dreams to Directives

The brilliance of dreams often dazzles the eyes, casting an enchanting spell of 'What Could Be.' Each aspiration feels tantalizingly possible in the mind's theater. Yet, it's one thing to dream, it's entirely another to bring those dreams down to the rugged terrain of reality, giving them shape and purpose.

Each dream requires a blueprint. Imagine standing at the foot of a mountain, its peak shrouded in mists of possibility. The path upward isn't always visible from the base, but with careful planning and mapping, each step becomes intentional, and the journey, navigable.

Growing up, I often gazed at the opulent ceiling above me, glistening with the shine of gold leaf. I was in a cocoon of privilege, surrounded by the kind of luxury that made every desire and comfort immediately accessible. The tales of uphill career battles, long office hours, and the relentless pursuit of professional dreams seemed like stories from another universe.

Years sped by, and soon I found myself walking the hallowed halls of a renowned Bschool. The ivory towers of my childhood were replaced with libraries brimming with knowledge, and lecture halls echoing with the ambitions of future leaders. Days seamlessly melted into nights, each hour marked by the thirst for knowledge, the rush of group projects, and the shared dreams of a cohort eager to imprint their mark on the world.

One such day, I found myself amidst a group of peers, each one animatedly discussing the day's lecture. Our professor, an astute observer known for his razor-sharp wit, approached our circle. Glancing in my direction, a playful smirk tugged at the corner of his mouth. "From a CDO today, to a CEO tomorrow, perhaps?" he mused aloud, referencing my newly earned badge of honor as the Customer Development Officer at Colgate-Palmolive.

His comment wasn't a mere jest meant for lighthearted banter. It resonated, like a gong echoing in the vast canyon. The gravity of his words wasn't about the title itself, but rather the sprawling, challenging path it mapped out. Intrigued and slightly overwhelmed, I turned to what I knew best: books. Like a miner digging for gold, I delved deep into the biographies of industry magnates, pioneers, and trailblazers, hoping to decipher the secret sauce behind their meteoric rises. As I turned page after page, a recurring theme emerged, one that countless legends before me had harnessed to their advantage -the relentless, unforgiving, yet immensely rewarding march of time.

By June 2011, the bustling corridors of Colgate became a familiar territory for me. Each morning, as I stepped into the office, a fresh set of challenges greeted me. With every challenge came invaluable lessons, many of which I scribbled down in my notebook or mentally bookmarked for future reference. Days transformed into weeks, and as the leaves began to change, signaling the onset of October, I couldn't help but notice an underlying rhythm to the corporate world.

The company, a titan in its industry, operated much like a well-oiled machine. There was a distinct cadence to its workings. While the earlier parts of the year were marked by a steady hum of activity, as the calendar pages flipped closer to December, there was a palpable increase in energy. Desks piled up with reports, meeting rooms echoed with animated discussions, and late-night lights at the office became more common. This crescendo was not merely about wrapping up annual projects, it was the anticipation of yearend reviews, of accolades, of a spotlight on those who had shone the brightest.

The 1231 Framework

It was in this electric atmosphere that the contours of my 1231 framework began to take shape. I realized that to truly thrive in this environment, I needed more than just instinct; I needed a strategy, a blueprint to guide my every goal and move.

The '1' in my framework stood as a sentinel for my monthly aspirations. These were immediate, tangible goals. Every 30 days or so, I would pause, taking a moment to reflect on my journey, celebrate my wins, and adjust my sails if I found myself veering off course.

Then came the '3', representing the trinity of connections, collaborations, and communication. Each quarter, I aimed to foster relationships, both within and outside my department. This wasn't just about networking, it was about forging genuine bonds. I envisioned a workspace where my peers would not just recognize my face, but also appreciate the value I brought to the table. I wanted to be more than just another name in an email thread; I aspired to be the colleague others could lean on, laugh with, and most importantly, trust.

Lastly, the '12' served as a panoramic lens, allowing me to view the entire year in its sprawling glory. This was where I charted out my broader ambitions. Be it devouring the latest bestsellers to stay abreast of industry trends, enrolling in courses to sharpen my skills, or satiating my wanderlust by hopping across continents to 19 different countries.

As I refined my 1231 framework at Colgate, I realized the profound impact of strategic planning on career progression. This personalized framework was the genesis of a more holistic approach, one that I came to call the Career Ascension Roadmap.

The Career Ascension Roadmap

The Visionary Canvas

Recall the words of Antoine de SaintExupéry: "A goal without a plan is just a wish." Your career is an intricate web, not of mere jobs and designations, but of aspirations, ambitions, and purpose. When you are charting unexplored territories, your map isn't filled with towns or cities but with milestones you want to achieve, challenges you aim to surmount, and the legacy you wish to etch. Dive beyond the superficial.

What realms do you wish to conquer? In which projects do you see your mark? What footprints will you leave for future explorers? With this envisioned map in hand, you have a compass that not only indicates where you are but more crucially, points to where you need to be. It becomes the bedrock upon which every subsequent decision, every step, and every venture is grounded, ensuring that even amidst the fiercest storms, you remain unerringly on course.

Your Tactical Blueprint

Every ambitious edifice begins with a blueprint. It's an architect's guiding document, charting out each step, predicting challenges, and laying down solutions. With your envisioned canvas in place, you now need to get tactical. What are the steps required to turn that dream into a reality? Here's where SMART objectives come into play. For example, if you see leadership in your future, narrow it down.

Do you want to be the person strategizing groundbreaking campaigns for a marketing department by the close of 2025? Such specificity transforms vague ambitions into tangible targets. These objectives then become the milestones, the markers on your roadmap, giving you short-term goals to achieve as you advance toward your ultimate career vision.

The Skill Inventory

Imagine an artisan in a workshop, surrounded by an array of tools. He knows each one intimately which chisel can carve the finest details, which hammer is best for broad strokes. Similarly, within you lies an array of skills and competencies. Some are razor sharp, ready to be wielded at a moment's notice. Others, perhaps, are a tad rusty and need some polishing. And, inevitably, there will be tools you don't yet possess but will need for the journey ahead. Taking stock isn't a mere administrative task; it's an introspective journey. By recognizing your strengths, you can leverage them, ensuring they're at the forefront of your professional narrative. Meanwhile, by identifying areas of growth, you remain ever-prepared, equipping yourself with the arsenal necessary to meet future challenges head-on.

Commit to Learning

The landscape of any industry is evolving, with new horizons constantly emerging. Just as a river adapts and carves its path, so too must we continuously shape and enrich our knowledge. It's not just about filling gaps—it's about adding depth and breadth to our understanding. Seek out those workshops that ignite your passion, enroll in courses that challenge your thinking, and chase those certifications that elevate your credibility. The pursuit of knowledge isn't a sprint; it's a marathon—a relentless, rewarding journey.

Feedback Loop

In the words of James Joyce, "Mistakes are the portals of discovery." But how do we recognize these portals? The answer lies in seeking feedback. Constructive criticism isn't just a mirror reflecting our present; it's a compass, directing our future growth. Embrace external viewpoints—they offer a panorama, a full-circle insight into how you're perceived, where you shine, and where the shadows of improvement lie. In essence, it's this continual reflection and refinement that crafts mastery.

Strategic Networking

There's a world out there brimming with untapped potential, waiting to be discovered. Every individual you meet is a doorway to a new opportunity, a new perspective, a new lesson. The power of networking isn't just in the number of hands you shake but in the genuine relationships you nurture. Whether it's at seminars where minds buzz with innovation or on digital platforms where ideas know no boundaries, weaving a network isn't about casting the widest net, but about creating meaningful, enduring connections that illuminate the path of possibility.

Visibility Plan

Imagine pouring your dedication and passion into a project, each detail meticulously crafted, every challenge meticulously overcome. Now, it's time to let that commitment shine, not draped in boastfulness, but as a testament to your dedication and the value you bring. Every hard-earned achievement deserves its moment in the spotlight. By ensuring your efforts are recognized, you don't just elevate your own journey but inspire and ignite the potential in those around you.

Adapt & Evolve

The world doesn't pause; it evolves, twists, and turns in unexpected ways. And while many tread cautiously, afraid of stumbling on the unexpected curves, there are those like you. You don't just adapt; you dance with change, rhythmically swaying, mastering every new beat that comes your way. This agility doesn't just set you apart; it places you at the forefront, writing the next chapter while others are still deciphering the last.

Brand Yourself

There's an undercurrent to our professional lives that's sometimes more profound than the overt accomplishments on our resumes—it's the subtle, memorable imprints we leave on others. A few years back, I found myself mingling in a networking event, rubbing shoulders with myriad professionals, some of whom I'd previously worked with at Amazon. Amidst the usual exchanges about careers and roles, a few of them pointed out something intriguing. They remembered an email signature of mine, not for any grand statement, but because it sported a playful image of Batman next to my name. It was a minuscule detail, an almost whimsical addition, but it set me apart in their memories.

Insert the signature

As you curate your personal brand, understand that it's not always the loudest moments that echo; sometimes, it's the quiet, unexpected touches that leave the most lasting impressions.

Reflect & Reset

Sometimes, amidst the whirlwind of daily tasks and deadlines, we forget to truly check in with ourselves. It's like running a marathon without ever looking at the path beneath our feet. Take a step back, even if just for a moment. Feel the weight of your achievements, the joy in the small victories, and the lessons in the missteps. This isn't just about patting yourself on the back; it's about grounding yourself. Knowing where you've been can guide where you're headed next. So, when the path gets foggy, or when doubts creep in, use these moments of introspection to help you recalibrate and move forward with renewed clarity and purpose.

By mastering these distinct strategies for various situations, professionals can ensure they're not just reacting to challenges but proactively addressing them with the best-suited approach. Whether it's engaging externally or navigating the maze of professional challenges, a strategic, well-formed stance can be the difference between mere survival and career ascension.

The Career Ascension Roadmap we've journeyed through isn't just a series of steps—it's a testament to the transformative power of meticulously set goals. As we've delved deep, it's clear that career ascension isn't a random act but a crafted trajectory. Every turn, every milestone, is underscored by proactive foresight and continuous feedback.

Emerging from this understanding of realigning personal ambitions to broader objectives and drafting a career ascension roadmap, there's no story that stands out more glaringly than the incredible journey of Jeff Bezos. Let's venture into this illuminating case study, where a pivot in personal goals reshaped the retail landscape globally.

From Wall Street to Digital Marketplace: Jeff Bezos's Paradigm Shift

Picture Wall Street in the 1990s. Its streets pulsated with ambition, power suits, and ringing telephones. Amid this fervor, a keen-eyed financial analyst named Jeff Bezos was making waves. For many, the allure of Wall Street, with its undeniable charm and the scent of money, would be the endgame. But for Bezos, it was merely the prologue.

A startling statistic—a 2,300% annual increase in web usage—crossed his desk. To many, this was an interesting tidbit to discuss over a coffee break. But to Bezos, it was a clarion call echoing the possibilities of tomorrow. Mirroring the strategic foresight and proactive insights we discussed in our roadmap, Bezos didn't just see numbers; he glimpsed a burgeoning frontier.

Stretching beyond the boundaries of finance, he let his imagination roam. In the quiet moments before dawn or perhaps during a late-night brainstorm, Bezos sketched a list—a precursor to what would become the world's most influential online marketplace. Books, universal in their appeal and cumbersome for brick-and-mortar stores to completely stock, became his chosen torchbearer. The spark was ignited, and in that quiet, electrifying moment, the blueprint for Amazon crystallized.

What followed was nothing short of a revolution. Amazon expanded its horizons, bit by bit, challenging norms, pioneering new experiences, and reimagining e-commerce. From a simple online bookstore, it morphed into a behemoth that touched every facet of the consumer's life.

The Bezos saga isn't just an entrepreneurial fairy tale. It's a testament to boundless vision. Instead of resting on his laurels in the concrete canyons of Wall Street, he saw himself spearheading an e-commerce vanguard. This narrative echoes the core principles we've dissected throughout our journey—the art of aligning individual fervor with seismic market shifts to create monumental legacies.

And what's the most compelling lesson in all this? Drawing parallels with our deep dive into fluidity and adaptability, Bezos reminds us that goals are dynamic entities. They shift, morph, and sometimes compel us to blaze entirely new trails.

Reflecting upon our Career Ascension Roadmap, Bezos emerges as a living, breathing paradigm. His meteoric ascent wasn't borne from mere chance—it was a choreographed dance of ambition and strategy, of tenacity converging with opportunity. It reinforces the conviction that the concepts and structures we've meticulously explored throughout our discussions aren't just textbook ideologies.

As the roadmap expands and evolves, so does our understanding of the indispensable role of goal setting. So, as we close this chapter, remember: the heights we achieve in our careers are directly proportional to the depth and clarity of our goals. Anticipate, adapt, and ascend, always guided by the light of well-defined objectives.

02

The Dynamics of Modern Leadership

Picture this: A bustling interview room, where the glint of ambition is palpable in the air. A question pierces this tension, "Can you sell this pen?" On the surface, it might appear straightforward, even clichéd. Alike the subtle complexities of the corporate world, it's not just about the pen. It's a mirror, reflecting the depth of an individual's beliefs and values.

The corridors of leadership echo with a similar sentiment. It isn't merely about the title or the accolades. It's about a deeper resonance, an alignment with core values, and a potent vision.

Value Selling: At its essence, this is the heartbeat of leadership. It's the undercurrent that defines not just who we are, but how we lead. It's about resonating with values so profoundly that they become second nature, guiding decisions, shaping strategies, and influencing interactions.

Virtue Selling: While values might be the compass, virtues are the very footsteps in the journey of leadership. These are the non-negotiable qualities that distinguish leaders and inspire teams. Embracing these virtues is more than a strategic move, it's a testament to one's character.

In the midst of my own journey, I've sought solace in values like adaptability and an unwavering commitment to feedback. These weren't mere entries on a resume; they were the torchbearers of my professional journey. With these as my anchors, I fervently pursued the tenets of collaboration, honesty, and openness. It wasn't a dictum; it was a shared dream and a collective vision.

Identifying and Nurturing Essential Leadership Qualities for Growth

Consider a serene university classroom filled with fresh-faced students, where the syllabus includes laws of thermodynamics, meticulously penned by physicists of yore. With the chalkboard's screech, complex equations unravel, detailing energy conservation and the steady march of entropy. To most, these laws may seem worlds apart from the boardrooms and highrise offices. Yet, when one sifts through the layers, a resonance emerges. It's not merely about particles and energy; it's about the very fabric of leadership.

The First Law, often discussed in hushed reverence, reminds us that energy is merely transferred and transformed, never lost. When we stand on the precipice of our nascent careers, there's an untamed energy within, akin to a dam waiting to be unleashed. When a clear leadership vision is absent, this reservoir may overflow aimlessly, its potential lost in torrents. But, with foresight and intent, this energy can be channeled.

Drawing parallels with the Second Law, we find that entropy, or the drift towards chaos, is an inherent trait of the universe. Analogously, careers can often start with crystalline clarity, only to devolve into disorder if unchecked. But with the light of leadership qualities illuminating the path early on, there's a method to the madness. We're no longer sifting through jumbled puzzle pieces in dim light; we're crafting achievements under the spotlight of purpose and direction.

Why journey through this labyrinth of physics and leadership, you ask? Because understanding these laws is akin to holding a compass in an ever-shifting landscape. It's about harnessing the raw fervor of one's early career days, steering it with purpose, and ensuring that, amidst career challenges, we're not just afloat but treading with precision.

The Leadership Lattice Framework

Amid the constant hum of the corporate world, where aspirations intertwine with cutthroat competition, certain tenets emerge, illuminating the path to leadership that's not just effective, but transformative. Let's delve into this Leadership Lattice Framework, reminiscent of intricate patterns on a lattice, where each component, though unique, contributes to a captivating whole.

Emotional Intelligence (EQ)

Picture the corporate sphere as a bustling metropolis. The streets are lined with towering ambitions, the air thick with the weight of aspirations. In this very landscape, Emotional Intelligence isn't just a skill; it's the lifeblood coursing through the veins of every true leader. It's the bridge connecting ambition with understanding, initiative with empathy. With high EQ, a leader doesn't merely navigate the corporate maze but understands its intricate patterns, foreseeing turns and avoiding dead ends.

Visionary Pragmatism

Vision without action is a dream, and action without vision is a nightmare. As leaders take the helm, they are expected to gaze at the horizon, envisioning the vast potential. Yet, this vision isn't woven from the threads of mere fantasies. It's anchored in reality, buttressed by pragmatism.

The legacy of Jack Ma, the brain behind Alibaba, exemplifies this quality. In the late 90s, when the internet was still nascent in China, Ma saw a world interconnected digitally. But his vision wasn't just of a China transformation; it was of a global digital marketplace. Naysayers were plenty, hurdles even more. Yet, he was not only tenacious in his dream but also astutely aware of the ground realities. With a fine balance of his expansive vision and grounded strategies, Ma transformed a dream etched in his apartment into a global e-commerce titan.

Decision-Making Prowess

At a major tech company, the CEO faced a monumental decision: to pivot their primary service offering or stick to their well-established route. Market trends suggested a paradigm shift, but initial user feedback on potential changes was mixed. The CEO, leveraging her decision-making prowess, initiated a deep dive into both quantitative data and qualitative insights. Organizing brainstorming sessions with her team, she gathered diverse perspectives. This amalgamation of intuition, team insights, and market data led to a phased pivot strategy. The result was a significant boost in user engagement and a renewed company direction that harmonized with the shifting digital landscape.

Resilience

Resilience, in the corporate sphere, is more than just bouncing back—it's about forging ahead, even in the face of adversity. Resilient leaders are characterized by their ability to anticipate disruptions, adapt to events, and create lasting value in tumultuous times. They possess an uncanny knack for seeing setbacks not as insurmountable obstacles, but as lessons, ever ready to recalibrate and redefine their strategies. This resilience is what sets apart companies that merely survive challenges from those that leverage challenges as springboards to greater heights.

Continuous Learning

In a world that's rapidly evolving, the ability to continuously learn is the wind beneath a leader's wings. Today's leaders must be in a perpetual state of learning, ensuring they're abreast of the latest innovations and shifts in the industry landscape. Continuous learning isn't just about personal growth—it's about ensuring the organization remains at the cutting edge, primed to harness new opportunities and confront challenges head-on. Leaders who champion learning foster cultures of curiosity, where questions are encouraged, knowledge is shared, and the pursuit of excellence never ceases.

Stepping forth from the rich insights of the Leadership Lattice Framework, my journey through the corporate world has been one of exploration across diverse terrains. From the dynamic corridors of FMCG and E-commerce to the pulsating hubs of Startups, Pharmaceuticals, Hospitality, and the innovative realm of the SaaS industry, every phase presented its unique set of challenges. Yet, amidst these multifaceted scenarios, one persistent aspect emerged the unwavering essence of leadership.

In every industry, despite the distinct challenges, the foundational qualities of leadership—vision, decision-making, collaboration, and resilience—remained steadfast, echoing the same values irrespective of the external landscape. Embracing this enduring principle, I diligently honed these leadership attributes, allowing them to guide me through each twist, turn, and tidal wave.

A defining moment crystallized during my tenure at Reckitt. As the quarter's conclusion loomed, our team, encompassing my peers and me, found itself at a crucial juncture. The conventional path seemed the obvious choice, yet I was compelled to venture beyond it. Engaging in a comprehensive dialogue with our sales team, I unearthed ground-level insights that often remained beneath the surface. A significant revelation highlighted the evolution of medical stores, now showcasing a broader range of products beyond just pharmaceuticals. Grasping this trend's potential, we recalibrated our strategy, resulting in not just bolstered revenue, but a renewed sense of purpose and enthusiasm within the team.

Later, during a chapter on a Hospitality Startup, the obstacle of escalating online customer acquisition costs presented itself. A seemingly innocuous conversation illuminated a potential avenue—India's prolific wedding industry. With an impressive count of wedding celebrations annually, the consequential demand for travel and accommodations was evident. Aligning with this insight, we forged collaborations with wedding venues, transforming them into strategic allies. This maneuver surged our revenue by 30% and brought forth recognition, marking me as the "Best Hub of the Quarter" within my initial tenure as the Hub Head of South India.

Upon introspection, these experiences serve as a testament to a core belief: while industries may vary in their nuances, the essence of leadership consistently remains a cornerstone for success and career ascension.

The Art of Fluid Leadership: Navigating the Spectrum Across Varied Career Stages

Leadership is a journey, not toward a static endpoint, but through evolving challenges and opportunities. As the winds and terrains change, so must the approach. Let's demystify the influential styles steering this expedition.

At its heart, leadership is about understanding and connecting. It is ever-fluid, informed by both innate tendencies and learned experiences. The challenge, and indeed the art, lies in discerning when to lean into a particular approach, understanding the nuances of each moment, and acting with deliberate intention.

The trajectory of one's career is not linear. Each juncture, each bend, each high, and each low carries with it a unique demand. In the early stages, you might need to be more direct, embedding yourself into the granular details. Yet, as you climb the ladder, the canvas broadens. The view becomes expansive, requiring them to zoom out, see patterns, connect dots, and set larger visions.

Every leader harbors a natural style, a default setting. However, the hallmarks of standout leadership lie in the finesse to harmonize this innate style with the external demands of each situation. It's like a skilled pianist, seamlessly moving from one note to another, ensuring the melody remains both consistent and captivating.

Take, for instance, the illustrious trajectories of Arianna Huffington and Brian Chesky.

Arianna Huffington, before she was the media mogul known for The Huffington Post, was a writer. Yet, as she ventured into the uncharted territories of digital journalism, her leadership demeanor underwent a transformation. Adapting to the fast-paced rhythm of the online world, she molded her style. And just when one thought they had her figured out, she transitioned to champion wellbeing through Thrive Global, echoing her prowess in adapting to divergent arenas.

On the other hand, Brian Chesky, Airbnb's cofounder, started with a mindset deeply entrenched in design. Yet, as Airbnb evolved from a fledgling idea into a global phenomenon, so did Chesky's leadership. He transitioned from focusing on intimate user experiences to spearheading macro strategies befitting a global CEO. His journey wasn't about abandoning his roots but about intertwining them with the broader oaks of leadership.

These narratives are more than just success stories. They're illustrative of the essence of fluid leadership. They underscore the need to be attuned to one's surroundings, to one's own evolution, and, importantly, to the silent, sometimes unacknowledged needs of their teams.

As the stories of Huffington and Chesky illuminate the ethos of fluid leadership, our sights are drawn to another emblematic figure who embodies this principle—Satya Nadella. His tenure at Microsoft serves as an exquisite portrayal of a leader who understands the duality of anchoring in one's strengths and embracing transformative winds.

Satya Nadella's Leadership at Microsoft: Breathing Fresh Life into a Tech Titan

Satya Nadella's journey isn't just about leading one of the world's premier tech giants; it's a tale of reinvention, both personal and institutional. When one dives into the annals of Microsoft's history, the era before Nadella seems like a different epoch, marked with its own set of achievements, but also weighed down by legacy baggage.

Nadella didn't just parachute into the CEO's office; he was a product of Microsoft's culture, having spent over two decades within its walls. Yet, his ascent wasn't merely due to his tenure. It was the synthesis of his deep technical expertise with his broader vision for what Microsoft could become.

As he climbed the echelons, Nadella always displayed an uncanny ability to discern where the technological winds were blowing. He recognized early on the paradigm shift from a 'know it all' to a 'learn it all' culture. Rather than rest on the laurels of Microsoft's past successes, he fostered a mindset of continuous learning, a shift from hubris to humility. It wasn't just about climbing the next hill, but understanding which hill to climb.

Under Nadella, Microsoft underwent a renaissance of sorts. While the world had perceived it as a fading star amid the rising luminance of newer tech entities, Nadella envisioned a different narrative. The company's pivot to cloud computing with Azure, the audacious acquisitions like LinkedIn and GitHub, and the rekindling of its commitment to open source reflected a Microsoft that was agile, receptive, and transformative.

But more than just strategic shifts, Nadella ushered in a cultural reawakening. He emphasized empathy, not just as a personal virtue but as a business imperative. For him, innovation sprouted from the ability to understand the unmet, unarticulated needs of customers.

To reflect upon Nadella's journey is to witness the art of leadership in its finest form. A leadership style that isn't rigid, but one that ebbs and flows with the demands of the times, all the while keeping its essence intact. As we delve further into the realms of leadership, Nadella's narrative stands as a testament: true leadership is not about where you start but the transformative journey you chart.

The richness of a leader's journey is enhanced by their ability to stand at the crossroads of introspection and feedback. Harnessing the right tools and frameworks for self-assessment becomes the foundation of this introspective process. It's not just about knowing where you stand but understanding the nuances that can elevate your leadership prowess to greater heights.

Yet, self-reflection, as vital as it is, gains an added dimension when supplemented with external perspectives. Enter the role of 360-degree evaluations. This comprehensive feedback approach unveils blind spots, accentuates strengths, and offers a panoramic view of one's leadership impact. It's akin to understanding the ripple effects of a stone thrown in a pond. The insights gained aren't just about the immediate point of impact but the wider ramifications.

And as we gather these layers of self and external insights, the journey doesn't conclude. Instead, it transitions into a phase of continuous improvement. Leaders, aspirants, and career enthusiasts must embrace the cycle of setting benchmarks, establishing goals, and steering their leadership evolution in tandem with their vision for career growth.

This melding of introspection, feedback, and relentless refinement is the alchemy of genuine career progression.

03

The Art of Effective Communication

Envision the pulse of conversations echoing through the corridors of an office space. Amidst the hum of dialogues and the whispers of deliberation, a battlefield of words and ideas unfolds. Here, your voice emerges as the hero, cutting through the cacophony with crystal clear clarity, wading through diverse thoughts and viewpoints.

Remember the teachings of Dale Carnegie, from his classic "How to Win Friends and Influence People." He spoke of the magic that unfolds when we genuinely see the world from another's perspective. Imagine a conversation where grace isn't just a virtue but a guiding principle. A dialogue where true listening creates an intimate dance between speaker and listener, and empathy reigns supreme over mere opinions.

Imagine a scenario where a young, ambitious manager is faced with the task of speaking to a group of seasoned professionals. Initially, she faced a daunting challenge: addressing a room of experienced professionals while feeling unprepared and unsure of her approach. Recognizing the need for a more structured and impactful method, she turned to the teachings of psychologist Robert B. Cialdini. His principles – like reciprocity, commitment, and social proof – offered a framework that she could apply in her communication.

She diligently studied these concepts, understanding how they could transform her approach from uncertain to confident. By incorporating the idea of reciprocity, she learned to create a sense of mutual exchange and respect with her audience. The principle of commitment helped her articulate her vision in a way that compelled her listeners to buy into her ideas. And through understanding social proof, she could strengthen her arguments with widely accepted ideas, making her points more persuasive.

As she spoke to the room, her newfound preparation was evident. Every word and concept was strategically chosen, based on Cialdini's principles, to craft a narrative that resonated with her audience. This structured approach, guided by psychological insights, turned her initial apprehension into a commanding presence, earning her the appreciation and respect of the experienced professionals.

By internalizing and embodying these teachings, individuals amplify their influence, ensuring their voice doesn't just add to the noise but resonates, is remembered, and is revered.

Steve Jobs & Apple's Resurgence: Navigating Resistance Through Profound Communication

The return of Steve Jobs to Apple in the late 1990s wasn't just a landmark event in the world of business, it was a masterclass in navigating resistance, subtle and overt. The challenges he faced weren't merely external market forces; they were also internal apprehensions, doubts, and silent disagreements.

Recognizing the Unstated Resistance

Beyond the stated challenges, Jobs faced an undercurrent of unspoken resistance. He understood that sometimes resistance wasn't always voiced. A crossed arm, an averted gaze, or even a shift in tone – these nonverbal cues often spoke louder than words. Drawing upon the idea that a majority of our communication is nonverbal, Jobs became adept at reading the room. The corridors of Apple were rife with whispered concerns and unvoiced questions, but Jobs' ability to discern these silent disagreements and confront them was one of his many strengths.

Mastering the Pitch

In the midst of this environment, Jobs, with his impeccable ability to articulate a vision, spoke in a manner that was both direct and evocative. However, beyond his words, it was his attention to the finer details of communication that stood out. He was sensitive to the tonal variations that could hint at doubt or opposition. Every pause, every inflection in his voice, was purposefully employed to convey assurance and dispel skepticism.

Turning the Tide with Open Dialogue

Jobs championed the cause of open dialogue at Apple. He established spaces where employees felt seen and heard, where every concern, however minor, was addressed with gravity. It was this ethos of clarity, combined with his mastery over nonverbal communication, that began to clear the mist of uncertainty at Apple.

In this era of his leadership, Apple's presentations transformed. They weren't mere product launches; they became narratives, stories that melded emotion and function, stories that resonated deeply with its audience, rekindling a shared passion for the brand's vision.

Thus, as the Apple story unfolded under Jobs' stewardship, it became evident that genuine, insightful communication—infused with an understanding of both verbal and nonverbal cues—was at the heart of its revival.

As we move away from the era of Steve Jobs, I find myself starting an exploration into the deep impact of visual storytelling in professional settings. It's a journey beyond just words, where visual communication stands out as a strong force, driving career growth and innovative evolution. In this journey, the language of images and emotions speaks loudly, guiding the path of professional growth toward endless innovation and progress.

In the evolution from traditional whiteboards to digital dashboards, I've found the power of visual tools to be indispensable for effective communication. During my early education, I gravitated toward presentations overwriting. The brevity and visual appeal of presentations resonated with me, and I consistently incorporated two elements: a captivating theme and the language of numbers, which always appealed to organizational stakeholders. This approach set a solid foundation for me as an entry-level manager.

However, as I climbed the corporate ladder, the complexity of ideas and processes I dealt with grew exponentially. It was here that tools like Whimsical became invaluable. Whimsical allowed me to distill intricate processes, from SIPOC to SOPs, into easily digestible visual representations. During my tenure in the hospitality industry, we recognized that a hotel stay wasn't merely about luxury or convenience, it was an entire experience, encompassing every touchpoint from check-in to checkout.

We employed the SIPOC model to visualize this flow. By dissecting the guest experience, we pinpointed critical areas of focus: the initial aroma upon entering a room, the cleanliness of bed linens, the importance of explaining available facilities with a warm smile, and promptly addressing any grievances. This visual representation was instrumental in conveying these intricacies to our Guest Delight Officers. With this clarity, we monitored these touchpoints rigorously, leading to consistent month-on-month improvements. The result? Our hub ascended to the top position in quality ratings.

SIPOC - Diagram

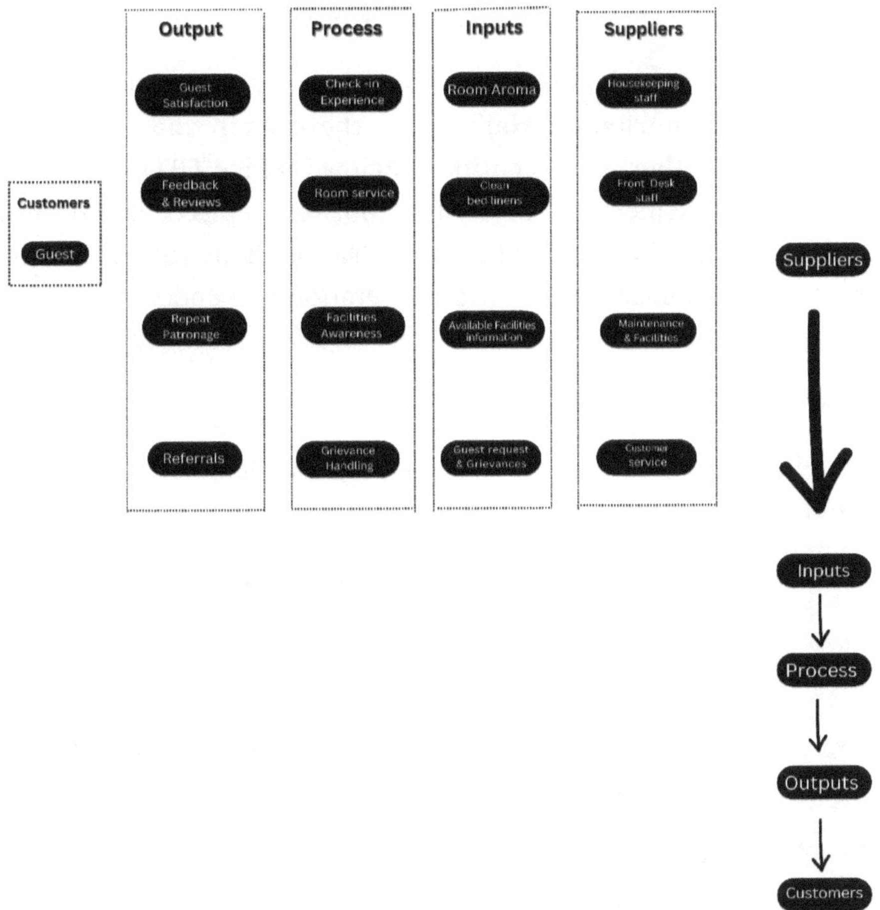

Such visualizations made a significant difference in how these ideas were received and understood by my peers and superiors. Another cornerstone of my approach to communication and idea management has been Evernote. For over eight years, this tool has been my constant companion, allowing me to capture fleeting ideas. As aptly mentioned in the book "Building a Second Brain," "Everything not saved will be lost." Our minds are designed for processing, not storage. Hence, it's crucial to save our ideas externally, ensuring they're not lost in the whirlwind of daily tasks and thoughts.

Navigating the Challenges of People: Speaking Their Language

WIIFM Horizontal for Individual Contributors

At the foundation of your professional journey, especially if you're an individual contributor, you're both the captain and the crew of your ship. Whether it's executing a BelowTheLine (BTL) marketing campaign, implementing a digital tool to replace cumbersome Excel sheets, or aiming to refine appraisal methods through an NPS survey, you're constantly seeking cooperation and endorsement from colleagues. They invariably ask: "What's In It For Me?" (WIIFM).

Happy Flow

Achieving your objectives often means aligning them with the interests of your peers:

- Give credit where it's due, highlighting their contribution through accolades.
- Emphasize the benefits of efficiency, such as the timesaving prospects of automation.
- Advocate for collective growth, as with improved appraisal methods through NPS feedback.

Flow of Feeling

However, there will be moments where resistance is met, often from those crucial to your objectives. In these situations:

- Maintain composure. Recognize that some resist change, not necessarily out of malice but possibly due to comfort with the status quo.
- Engage with mentors outside your immediate environment. Their perspective can offer strategies to bridge communication gaps.
- Avoid categorizing these individuals as 'difficult' in your mind. Instead, view them as unique challenges to learn from.

WIIFM Vertical Downwards for Early Managers

Ascending into a managerial role brings a shift in dynamics. You're now orchestrating a diverse team, each member with their distinct characteristics — be it their generational identity or their introverted/ extroverted nature.

Grasp the nuances of your team's makeup. Recognize that a Gen Z introvert might have different needs and communication preferences than a Gen Y extrovert.

Strike a balance in interaction. Determine the right frequency and modality, be it virtual or in person, to ensure consistent, effective communication without overwhelming or alienating your team.

The next layer of our roadmap emphasizes the importance of effectively communicating and aligning with those above you in the hierarchy.

Mastering the Vertical Upwards Communication: WIIFM (What's In It For Me?)

CEO's Interface with Key Stakeholders

Top-tier leaders, in adopting a CEO mindset, recognize the pivotal role of their relationships with investors, shareholders, and other key stakeholders in crafting their legacy. These interactions are crucial not only in defining their personal career paths but also in shaping the destiny of the organizations they lead. Understanding the WIIFM factor from the perspective of these stakeholders becomes an essential skill for any professional aspiring to make a significant impact at the highest levels.

Perfecting The Art of Texting

In our digital age, significant decisions often sprout from simple text on platforms like Slack or WhatsApp. Hence, mastering concise and impactful texting is essential. A well-crafted message can set the stage for more meaningful dialogues.

Crafting the '10-second Hook'

Early managers, remember this: time is a precious commodity for higher-ups. The ability to present your ideas compellingly in a short span can be the difference between approval and being overlooked. A real-life example is the Program Manager in a startup who navigated a challenging situation with his senior by aligning his proposal with what mattered most to the manager's potential profits. It's not just about conveying the idea, it's about presenting it in a language that resonates.

Starting with the End Goal

When charting out your plans or presentations, visualize the conclusion. By invoking Murphy's Law and preemptively considering potential pitfalls, you can anticipate challenges. Determine where you need support, especially when dealing with controllable and uncontrollable factors.

The Chameleon Mastery

The term 'chameleon' often bears a negative connotation in professional settings. But here, it's not about blind acquiescence or mindlessly pleasing superiors. It's about the art of adaptability. Every leader has their distinct leadership and communication style, rooted in their unique values and experiences. To effectively communicate and collaborate, it's crucial to align with this style without compromising one's integrity. Recognize, appreciate, and then harmonize with their mode of communication to ensure a seamless flow of ideas, goals, and feedback.

WIIFM Through the Prism of Visual Communication

The essence of effective communication, especially within the professional realm, lies in the art of distilling complex ideas into understandable visuals. This process, crucial for both individual contributors and managers, involves converting abstract concepts into actionable strategies.

The Art of Simplification: Echoing Steve Jobs' sentiment that simplicity is often harder than complexity, we recognize the challenge of breaking down intricate ideas. Inspired by works like Jeff bezo's "Amazon flywheel in the napkin", we see the power of simple drawings in communicating complex ideas across diverse audiences.

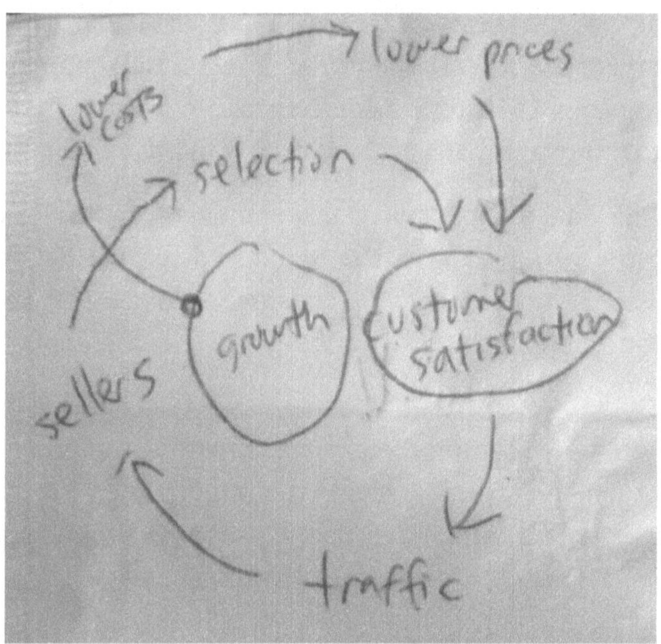

Strategies for Visual Simplicity

Adopt a Uniform Visual Language: Using consistent symbols, charts, and colors enhances clarity and reduces confusion.

Focus on the Core Message: Trimming excess details to spotlight the central idea helps maintain the audience's focus.

Utilize Advanced Visual Tools: Tools like Whimsical, Canva, or Adobe Spark offer creative ways to present complex ideas in an impactful manner.

Embrace Iteration and Feedback: Continuously refine visuals to achieve clarity and effectiveness.

Decoding Indra Nooyi's Leadership Through the Lens of WIIFM

In the bustling corridors of global business, Indra Nooyi's name often resonates with a particular clarity. Her tenure at PepsiCo was marked not just by traditional success but by a profound, empathetic approach to leadership. At the heart of it? A keen understanding of the subtle "What's In It For Me?" (WIIFM) principle, essential for anyone striving to connect, lead, and inspire. Let's embark on a journey, delving into Nooyi's leadership approach and its transformative effect on PepsiCo.

Nooyi's magic lay in her ability to genuinely connect. Rather than imposing top-down mandates, she tuned into the WIIFM frequencies of employees, stakeholders, and consumers alike. She transformed PepsiCo from just another corporate giant into a community where every voice mattered.

For those at the onset of their careers, Nooyi's approach offers a goldmine of insights. It underscores the importance of seeing beyond one's immediate role, understanding what drives others, and aligning those motivations with overarching organizational goals.

One particularly endearing chapter from Nooyi's leadership story is her thoughtful gesture of writing letters to her executives' parents. This wasn't for show. It was a genuine acknowledgment of the broader influences and backgrounds that shape an individual's professional journey.

But her efforts went beyond touching gestures. She set the stage for a company culture defined by mutual respect, understanding, and shared purpose. It's a potent reminder of how genuine, open communication can reshape organizational dynamics.

Under Nooyi's watch, terms like diversity and inclusion were elevated from corporate jargon to actionable agendas. They became central pillars of PepsiCo's identity. Her unwavering commitment to elevating diverse voices, particularly those of women and marginalized groups, stands as a testament to her vision of a dynamic and inclusive workplace. Recognizing the unique dynamics of her team, much like understanding the differences between a Gen Z introvert and a Gen Y extrovert, she crafted an environment that resonated with inclusion at every turn.

Indra Nooyi's tenacity at PepsiCo wasn't just about changing a product line; it was about reading the evolving needs of consumers and reflecting on the broader societal shift. The market was demanding healthier options, and Nooyi, ever the forwardthinker, was swift to recognize this. She steered the beverage giant in a direction that many would have found risky, but her instincts were spot on. The company's net revenue surged impressively by 26%. It wasn't merely an adaptation; it was a proactive realignment.

Remember the earlier emphasis on mastering the "Vertical Upwards Communication: WIIFM"? Nooyi exemplified this by aligning her strategies with the broader objectives of PepsiCo, appealing to shareholders, stakeholders, and, most importantly, the consumers. Her moves always had an unmistakable stamp of 'What's In It For Me?' for all parties involved.

This wasn't a standalone strategy. Much like the earlier mentioned "10second Hook," her decisions were often bold, and assertive, yet perfectly timed to capture the attention and allegiance of those around her. A notable practice of hers, writing personal letters to the parents of her executives, might seem detached from business strategy. Yet, it served as a potent tool, integrating the essence of the 'WIIFM Vertical Downwards for Early Managers' approach. By connecting at such a profound level, she wasn't just communicating; she was fostering an atmosphere brimming with respect, understanding, and collaborative spirit.

For budding professionals and seasoned managers alike, the essence of Nooyi's leadership serves as a roadmap. Not just for success, but for forging meaningful relationships, understanding and anticipating change, and driving growth with a heart. Through her journey, Nooyi teaches us that leadership isn't merely about the climb; it's also about how you touch lives along the ascent.

When Words Meet Action: Leadership Beyond Rhetoric

Taking a leaf from Indra Nooyi's leadership journey, a clear message resonates: True leadership is not just about eloquent speeches; it's about genuine actions that validate those words. Nooyi wasn't one to just articulate lofty ideals. She put those principles into practice, showing the world the power of authentic connection and the transformation it brings.

Thinking back to my Bschool days, I recall managing massive events with constrained resources. More than just a task, it was an invaluable lesson in trust. It became evident that grand speeches or impressive visions aren't the sole drivers for commitment. People resonate with leaders who don't just speak but actively embody their beliefs. They seek figures who, beyond words, demonstrate true dedication through their actions.

Venture into the intricate fabric of any organizational culture, and you find a diverse group of individuals, each contributing their unique strengths and experiences. Herein lies the significance of Rewards, Recognition, and Remuneration. Taking cues from the 'WIIFM Vertical Downwards' approach, it's evident that genuine recognition, simple as it may sound, often holds the key. A timely acknowledgment, a mere nod of appreciation, can mean the world. Yet, it's surprising how often leaders choose grand gestures over these genuine moments of connection.

My experience at Prione, before its integration with Amazon, threw me into the deep end of this leadership conundrum. Tasked with pioneering fresh ventures, I wasn't just wearing the hat of a commander; I was more of a mentor, a guide. With a vast team that was as diverse as it was talented, the challenge was clear: create a space where every voice matters, and every effort shines.

It was during this period that the "Nation Wants to Know" campaign sparked to life. It wasn't just another organizational initiative, it became our rallying cry, a platform where achievements weren't merely highlighted—they became shared stories of passion, dedication, and collective success.

True leadership, in any setting, is rooted in empathy. But empathy is not just about understanding; it's about translating those feelings into tangible actions that uplift all. Reflecting on Nooyi's transformative leadership or drawing from my personal journey, one conviction stands unshaken: Genuine leadership manifests when words take flight through authentic actions. When this alignment is achieved, it becomes the bedrock for thriving individuals and flourishing organizations.

04

Synergy in Action

Do you remember those moments when you and your friends tried to do something on your own, only to realize the effort was easier and more rewarding when done together? Well, the corporate world isn't much different. I've always believed that at the heart of every professional success lies collaboration.

During the initial stages of my career, there was Vijay. His desk, littered with coffee mugs and endless sticky notes, was a few feet away from mine. But the clutter was deceptive. It didn't define him, but his stories did. We'd often end up sharing lunch where Vijay would invariably narrate an intriguing anecdote from his past.

Once, he told me about a large boulder blocking the entrance of a park in his childhood neighborhood. Every child took turns trying to push the stubborn rock away. All solo attempts, no matter how spirited, failed. It was only when they pooled their energies, standing shoulder to shoulder, did that boulder roll away.

With a chuckle, Vijay leaned in and whispered, "Sounds familiar, doesn't it? In our jobs, we tackle 'rocks' every day. Alone, it's an uphill battle. But together? That's where the magic happens." The essence of his words resonated deeply. The journey from considering colleagues as mere co-travelers to viewing them as invaluable allies in our professional journey is a game-changer.

Colleagues are more than just faces we see during meetings or names in our inboxes. They're allies, fellow trailblazers, each holding a piece of the puzzle. At the heart of it, fostering a partnership spirit is about recognizing that while individual goals set our compass, it's the shared passion, mutual respect, and collective drive that propel us forward.

Valuing Every Voice: Drawing from Best Practices to Promote Open Dialogue

I often spend a few minutes after a tiring day sitting under the night sky. As I gaze up, I see the countless stars, each glowing with its own tale. That's a lot like the world of business. There are countless stars – professionals, each with a unique story, each shining in their own right. But isn't there always that one star that outshines the rest? The one that makes you think, "That's not just a star; that's a supernova!"

Imagine walking into an immense conference hall. The air is thick with anticipation. Chatter fills the room, ranging from the enthusiastic intern, still green behind the ears but with eyes filled with dreams, to the seasoned executive. His stories? They're legendary, whispered in hushed tones during coffee breaks. Amidst this hum, it isn't the loudest voice that stands out. No, it's the voice that carries a story, a purpose, an echo of authenticity.

At these symposiums, it's easy to spot those trying to shout over the crowd, mistaking volume for value. Yet, the real magic lies with those who've learned a different tune.. It's less about speaking and more about connecting.

This kind of discernment, this nuanced understanding of communication, is vital in the corporate jungle. Where opportunities loom large, challenges intertwine like creeping vines, and crossroads of decision-making become the norm. So, how does one go about this complex space without losing their way?

Well, there are three neon signs pointing the way: The 1231 framework, the unmistakable glow of WIIFM (What's In It For Me), and the unmissable billboard that reads "Talk the talk, walk the walk". Together, they form the lanes of the SIP approach: Sensibility, Intellect, and Popularity.

SIP – Sensibility, Intellect and Popularity

Now, Sensibility isn't merely about going by the book. It's about feeling the pulse of the place, much like a local who knows the best coffee spots in a city. Translate this to the boardroom, and it's about showcasing your ideas, not as mere slides, but as a reflection of your essence. And when you do? That's when heads turn in acknowledgment, and eyes light up in interest.

Intellect, on the other hand, can be considered as the high-speed metro, efficiently cutting through distances. Think about fast-tracking a year's journey into a whirlwind few months. Overwhelming? Absolutely. But that's what the 1231 framework nudges you towards. When you take that challenge head-on, you're not just another face in the crowd; you become the dynamo that electrifies every meeting, and every project.

Now, Popularity might sound like a high school popularity contest, but it's far from it. It's not about being known by everyone, but about being known for something. WIIFM reminds us that every interaction is an exchange of value. So, ask yourself: What value do you bring to the table? When you're the person who consistently offers a fresh outlook, solid expertise, or spark of innovation, you become the colleague everyone wants on speed dial.

I've had the privilege of meeting many remarkable individuals like Robert in my corporate life. But Robert still stands out in stark relief. He wasn't just good at what he did; he lived and breathed the SIP paradigm.

What set Robert apart wasn't just raw talent. It was his unparalleled commitment. When projects seemed like mammoth mountains, where most saw dead ends, he saw challenges waiting to be conquered. His knack for navigating challenges didn't go unnoticed. His superiors, having witnessed his consistent brilliance, naturally leaned into a deep-rooted belief in his capabilities. This relationship between him and his leadership reminded me of the Pygmalion effect.

PYGMALION EFFECT

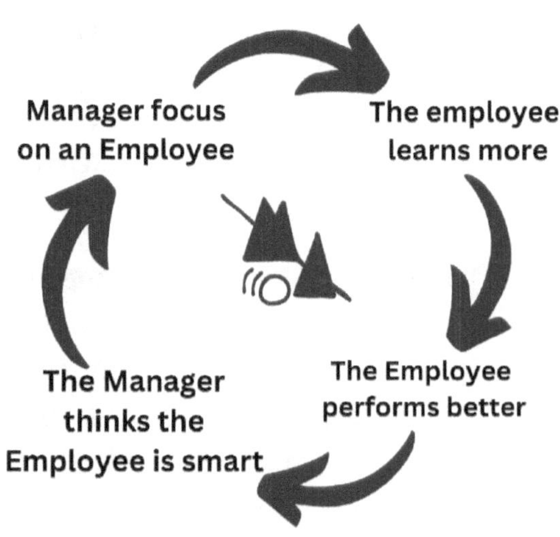

The Pygmalion effect isn't just a psychological term, it upholds the transformative power of belief. Just as the ancient Greek sculptor Pygmalion poured his heart into his work, willing his creation to spring to life, so too can leaders breathe life into their teams' potential by setting high expectations. When you're backed by such trust, not only do you strive to meet those expectations, but more often than not, you exceed them.

However, it's worth noting that Robert's journey wasn't about appeasing those above him. Recalling the concept of Chameleon Mastery we discussed in the previous chapters, you can realize that his journey was far from that. He never indulged in blind agreement or empty flattery. His approach was grounded in authenticity, showcasing genuine skill and vision. While hierarchy in an organization may set the stage, it's respect and genuine rapport that steal the show. In the end, it's not titles but trust, not positions but perceptions, that carve out a distinct path in the corporate world. And Robert? He's a living proof of that.

This ethos, which Robert so masterfully embraced, speaks to a larger truth that extends beyond the individual. It's a sentiment that cascades into the broader scope of an organization, shaping its very core.

The heartbeat of any organization isn't found in its infrastructure or its revenue streams but within the pulse of its teams. Teams—diverse, dynamic, and driven—are the lifeblood that fuels innovation and growth. But what transforms a group of individuals into a cohesive team?

Synergy.

It's the intangible magic that happens when the collective output is greater than the sum of individual efforts.

However, achieving synergy isn't as simple as putting together a group of talented individuals and expecting fireworks. It requires understanding, patience, and a deep commitment to fostering genuine connections.

KYC (Know Your Colleague): Deepening Understanding of Team Dynamics

You've likely heard of KYC in the banking sector—a thorough 'Know Your Customer' process to understand the client's nuances. But in the corporate world, there's another KYC that's equally important: Know Your Colleague.

Think about it. We spend a significant chunk of our lives at work. Yet, how much do we truly know about the person sitting next to us? Beyond their role and some weekend plans, how familiar are we with their aspirations, strengths, fears, or even their preferred style of communication? Knowing these can dramatically change the way we interact, collaborate, and build solutions together.

Deepening our understanding of team dynamics isn't just about being nosy or making small talk. It's about forging connections that are anchored in trust and empathy.

When we genuinely invest time and effort into knowing our colleagues— their working style, their motivators, their strengths, and areas they're keen to develop—we begin to see them in a new light. We move beyond surface-level interactions to a place where collaboration is intuitive and seamless. Differences no longer become roadblocks but rather catalysts for innovative solutions.

Embracing the KYC philosophy is the first step toward enhancing team synergy. It's about building bridges of understanding and fostering an environment where every member feels seen, valued, and heard. When teams operate from this place of deep connection and mutual respect, they don't just function—they flourish.

Championing Crossfunctional Collaboration: Dissolving Barriers

In today's corporate world, we often encounter walls. These walls, or 'silos,' stifle communication, hinder creativity, and obstruct the natural flow of ideas. But what if, instead of walls, we could build bridges?

Crossfunctional collaboration is the art and science of bridgebuilding in the corporate domain. It's not about mere token meetings or cursory exchanges. It's an attempt to tap into the reservoirs of diverse knowledge scattered across an organization.

So, how can a business leader or team manager champion such collaboration?

Dive Deep with Open Dialogue: Begin by creating a space that's devoid of judgment—a haven for ideas. Host regular brainstorming sessions, where teams can present their successes and challenges. When a marketer vocalizes the challenge of targeting a new demographic, a developer might offer an innovative tech solution, leading to a breakthrough campaign.

Action: Designate a bimonthly "Ideas & Innovations Day." Encourage every department to present a challenge they're facing and invite solutions from members of other teams.

Foster Fluidity with 'Educate & Rotate': The broader one's perspective, the richer the ideas they bring. By rotating team members across different functions, you're not just moving human resources but also transferring insights. When an IT professional spends time in HR, they might devise a tech solution to streamline recruitment. A sales executive in product development could provide firsthand insights into customer preferences.

Action: Initiate a "Role Rotation Program." Every quarter, allow team members to apply for a two-week stint in a different department of their choice, followed by a feedback session to share and implement learned insights.

Celebrate Collaborative Triumphs: In an ecosystem that often celebrates individual achievements, make it a point to spotlight collaborative successes. This boosts morale and cements the importance of cross-functional teamwork in the organizational culture.

Action: Introduce a "Collaborative Project of the Month" award. This isn't about the size or budget of the project but the extent of interdepartmental collaboration. Celebrate the team with a feature in the company newsletter or an exclusive lunch with the CEO.

Facilitate Constant Communication: It's essential to keep the lines of communication open even when there aren't any formal collaboration projects. Digital platforms like Slack or Microsoft Teams can be invaluable. Create dedicated channels for cross-departmental communications where teams can share updates, ask questions, or even celebrate minor victories.

Action: Set up a "CrossComm Channel" on your team communication platform. Encourage teams to post weekly updates and actively engage with posts from other departments.

With that thought, let's go back a bit.

My early days at Colgate were exciting and full of potential. I was the new kid on the block, eager to make a difference. Soon, an opportunity came knocking – an introduction to the Regional Program Head of Pharmacy Initiatives. The task? A curious blend of our products and the world of pharmaceutical distributors. For many, this was unfamiliar territory. Heck, even for me, it felt like I was handed a jigsaw puzzle with pieces from different boxes.

But here's the thing about challenges: they're opportunities in disguise. Instead of getting overwhelmed, I decided to sit down with both our teams and the distributors. We chatted, discussed challenges, and shared coffee-filled laughs. Before we knew it, we weren't just partners in a project, we were a team.

In our corporate life, there are moments that change everything. For me, it felt like standing at a pivotal crossroads, keenly aware that all our hard work was about to pay off.

Immersing myself in the project, I felt an overwhelming mix of excitement and apprehension. The thrill of learning something new, the challenge of unfamiliar terms like POC and PMF, was nothing short of an adventure. This was a hands-on, transformative experience, emphasizing the importance of grounding oneself, always learning, and always, always talking.

The Scholl Adventure

Here's another chapter I often replay. Out of the blue, without a roadmap or a big title, I was irresistibly drawn to the role of Program

POC for Scholl. Even though it was crafted with international audiences in mind, a voice inside told me it had a special place in India.

My luck turned when I bumped into a seasoned pro, an expert in both retail and foot care. What started as casual coffee chats soon morphed into spirited strategy sessions. Each discussion was a revelation, shedding light on the untapped potential that stretched from busy marketplaces to the broader health sector.

Of course, the journey wasn't smooth. Leading the Scholl charge meant diving deep into finances, understanding logistics, and liaising with countless distributors. Each challenge felt like a test of resolve. But that gut feeling—that we were onto something big—kept me going.

Three relentless months later, we had our answer. Our efforts reflected not just in sales figures but in the buzz, and the excitement, with a whopping 60% of outlets coming back for more. As our sales tally got a 3% boost, a personal highlight arrived: a nod of appreciation, recognizing me as the "Super Star" for the first half of 2014.

Aristotle's wisdom rings true in the most unexpected avenues of life, particularly when observing the dynamics of a team. Imagine a family, each person with a unique blend of eccentricities, strengths, and vulnerabilities. Yet, when combined, they create shared experiences, memories, and magic. This becomes especially vivid in my mind when I rewind to the Sri Lankan cricket team's astounding journey in 1996. Under the leadership of Arjuna Ranatunga, a team that might've been discounted by many, soared, proving that the spirit of unity can transform perceived weaknesses into triumphant strength.

My Meesho Journey like srilankan men's cricket in 1996

This memory often paints a backdrop to my own days at Meesho with the "Feet On Street" (FOS) team. At first glance, they seemed like the proverbial underdogs of a small battalion of twelve in the vast armies of the corporate world. But oh, how they grew. Under my stewardship, this modest squad metamorphosed, burgeoning into an imposing army of over 150 in a span as short as 6-8 months. Now, e-commerce, with its vast and intricate web, offers countless channels for seller acquisition. The pathways range from sleek websites to the agile terrains of performance marketing. Yet, in this digital landscape, the FOS approach felt almost anachronistic, but in a beautifully nostalgic way. Their mission wasn't just about numbers and transactions; it was about bridging worlds. They reached out to offline sellers, offering them a vision of the online marketplace, and inviting them to take a leap of faith.

But here's the poignant twist in the tale: this very team, whose core ethos was to instill trust and guide others towards change, grappled with trust issues within its own ranks.

As July 2020 dawned with the easing of lockdown measures, digital landscapes began to shimmer, signaling a boom. Every entrepreneur worth their salt knew that this was a moment of both challenge and colossal opportunity. And amidst this, our FOS team, though full of potential, faced its own set of tribulations. But I've always believed that sometimes, to find your way forward, you must look back.

Drawing from the experiences in the early chapters of my career, I championed the cause of grassroots insights. It's a lesson I've held close: Every organization, much like a story, has its quirks. But if amidst those intricacies, there's a narrative strength that sings louder than any flaw, then that's where the magic lies. Every feedback, every on-ground observation, no matter how minuscule, was treated as a gold nugget. With meticulous care, I made sure these nuggets were shared, ensuring that our leadership was not just informed but truly connected to our journey.

But merely gathering insights wasn't the endgame. I pivoted to honing processes, making them sharper, and more intuitive. Enter the scorecard system and a feedback loop. These weren't just tools but mirrors reflecting both the gleam of strengths and shadows of weaknesses.

Here's the catch, though: In the corporate space, it's so easy to strike the somber notes of weaknesses, often forgetting to celebrate the vibrant chords of strengths. Many a manager, with all good intentions, inadvertently dims the light of their teams by not shining a spotlight on their strengths. I resolved to sidestep this trap. I not only acknowledged but also celebrated my team in public forums.

The delicate strands of trust, while unseen, can construct the sturdiest bridges. Every ounce of effort I poured into illuminating our team's achievements—whether they be mere ripples or roaring waves—did not go unnoticed. I always made it a point to keep not only my immediate managers in the loop but also those a level above. By September, change was in the air. From the regional alleys, I found myself looking over the sprawling expanse of the nation, orchestrating the ambitious scaling of the FOS team. Think about it— from a humble team of a dozen, we mushroomed into a force of 150, all within the span of a fleeting six months. While the swelling numbers were heartening, this journey's soul lay in its deeper resonances—the acknowledgment, the applause. The shelves in my office gleamed with accolades, notably the "Burning Midnight Oil" and "Best Manager" awards. But more than these tangible tokens, the real reward was witnessing the metamorphosis of individual team members into champions, their voices becoming the medium of praises of our collective achievements.

Peeling back the layers, the core revelation from this adventure was profound. Mastering the pulse and rhythm of a team is not just about chart-topping successes. It's about celebrating every note, and realizing that in unity, we don't just add, we multiply, creating masterpieces far surpassing what any of us could have done in solitude.

Building on these triumphant notes, it's vital to reflect on the lessons these pivotal moments imbue us with. These tales of corporate adventures are more than just milestones, they offer invaluable insights that can shape our perspectives, guiding both our professional and personal journeys.

Lessons Carved in Experience

The Power of Vision

Your badge or business card might give you a title, but it's your vision that carves your legacy. It's easy to get bogged down by the day-to-day, but it's essential to lift your gaze, to see beyond the here and now. Whether you're a manager, an executive, or an intern, it's not the chair you occupy but the change you drive that truly counts. So, no matter where you're seated, always aim to get a panoramic view.

Fueling the Flame of Curiosity

Remember when we were kids, and the world was full of endless wonders? That innate curiosity is a gift, one we shouldn't shelve as we grow older. It's those burning questions, that insatiable thirst for knowledge, that can lead us down paths less traveled. maze, It's this curiosity that can unearth golden opportunities, lying in wait just beneath the surface.

Teaming Up for Triumph

We're in an era where silos are passé, and collaboration is the new king. The age-old ladders of hierarchy, while offering structure, can sometimes fence us in. Breaking these barriers, valuing input from every corner of the room, and fostering a spirit of true teamwork can lead to magic. When everyone feels heard and respected, resistance melts away, replaced by synchronized efforts marching towards a collective goal.

The strength of the team is each individual member. The strength of each member is the team. While the corporate ladder might give direction to some, real growth is more organic, and more human. It's found in the corners of rooms during casual conversations, in the middle of challenging projects, and in the heart of disagreements. It's there in our daily choices, in our willingness to champion our peers' strengths, and in our ability to adjust our sails based on mutual respect.

As for leadership? Influence isn't about the spotlight. It's about the shadows you cast when no one's watching. It's about the moments when you, without any external push, choose to lead with empathy, vision, and authenticity.

At this critical juncture, it is worth pondering: Are we just working together, or are we truly understanding, valuing, and growing with one another? Because therein lies the difference between a group of coworkers and a dynamically thriving team.

Leveraging Criticism and Feedback

Criticism is often the wildcard in the high-stakes game of professional advancement. Think about it: it can either unsettle your hand or, if played wisely, can become your trump card.Criticism, often perceived as a professional hazard, is in fact a vital tool for growth. Its dual nature serves both as a reality check and a guiding light. On one side, it can be a stark reflection of our weaknesses and areas in need of improvement. On the other, it serves as a catalyst, propelling us toward untapped potential and skill enhancement.

The art of leveraging criticism hinges on the ability to discern its nature — distinguishing the constructive from the destructive. Constructive criticism, often grounded in objective assessment, offers a treasure trove of actionable insights. It's the kind of feedback that, although it may be tough to swallow, provides clear pointers for improvement and growth. On the contrary, destructive criticism tends to lack a solid foundation, serving more as a source of demoralization rather than inspiration.

A blend of emotional intelligence and professional clarity is crucial here. It's about engaging in a dialogue with the feedback, asking critical questions such as, "How does this feedback align with my professional goals?" or "Is there a concrete, actionable element within this criticism?" This approach transforms criticism from a mere obstacle or source of discouragement into a valuable tool, building one's path to personal and professional development.

However, the journey doesn't end with merely distinguishing the type of criticism. The crux lies in responsive adaptation — an active and conscious engagement with the feedback received. This goes beyond the act of hearing to truly listening, beyond a knee-jerk reaction to thoughtful reflection, culminating in the integration of this feedback into one's professional ethos and practice. It calls for the creation of a dynamic plan, one that absorbs the essence of the criticism and aligns it with personal and career aspirations.

The 1% Ear's Duty: Heart and Head Framework

While many of us have mastered the art of acknowledging feedback, the journey from acknowledgment to action is less traversed. In the corporate corridors where interactions are laced with nuances and hierarchies, even a single sharp remark from a superior can resonate deeply, echoing far beyond the walls of the meeting room.

My own tryst with this reality began in the early days of my career in the FMCG sector, a field where market visits are as pivotal as client meetings in the tech industry. I recall a specific visit that involved a senior general manager, an event that drew significant attention across various levels of the company hierarchy. The scope of this visit was expansive, affecting not just my immediate area but the entire zone, state, and region, along with every stakeholder in the company.

Preparation for such visits is intense and multifaceted, involving meticulous engagement with distributors, ensuring our godowns were fully stocked, and that our products were prominently displayed across retail outlets. This wasn't just a routine part of the job, it was a performance, a display of our brand's strength and market presence. Despite thorough preparations, an undercurrent of anxiety persisted, not born of unpreparedness but from a deeply rooted fear of failure. This fear, similar to what a parent feels watching their child take tentative steps up a staircase, is a classic example of Risk Aversion, where the mind fixates more on potential pitfalls than on the prospects of success.

The visit, for the most part, was a success. Yet, in the unforgiving corporate world, it is often the smallest missteps that are magnified. In our case, it was a minor error – a product misplaced in a supermarket aisle. This slight but noticeable oversight brought forth a torrent of criticism from my superior, who didn't mince words in expressing his displeasure, labeling me a 'fool'. This label, harsh and jarring, cut through me. It highlighted a crucial aspect of professional life: we are conditioned to bask in the warmth of praise and recoil at the sting of criticism, often shutting our ears and hearts to it.

However, true professional growth demands a different approach. It requires cultivating what I like to call 'The 1% Ear's Duty' – a deliberate effort to listen, truly listen, to that 1% of criticism that holds the potential to catalyze significant personal and professional development. This approach is rooted in a 'Heart and Head Framework', a balanced methodology of processing feedback intellectually and emotionally.

The 2x2 Mind Map of Handling Feedback

The 'Heart and Head Framework' can be visualized through a 2x2 mind map, a strategic tool that guides us in dissecting and utilizing feedback.

TYPE OF FEEDBACK PROVIDERS

Constructive Mentor

Compassionate Supporter

Critical Analyst

Disconnected Director

The Balanced Approach: Harmonizing Emotional Acceptance with Rational Analysis

Feedback Giver: The Constructive Mentor

Imagine a mentor whose feedback is both a critique and a wellspring of growth-oriented advice. This approach is about striking a delicate balance between emotional acceptance and rational analysis. When faced with such feedback, the first step is to embrace it emotionally, acknowledging the mentor's intention to foster growth. This acceptance paves the way for a more objective, rational analysis. It's about dissecting the feedback, extracting actionable insights, and then crafting a plan that integrates this wisdom into your professional development. The response to such feedback is twofold: a sincere expression of gratitude for the mentor's insights, followed by a reflective phase where you assimilate and apply the advice to your work.

Emotional Resilience: Blending Emotional Acceptance with Rational Ignorance

Feedback Giver: The Compassionate Supporter

In this quadrant, the feedback giver plays the role of a compassionate supporter, intertwining support with critique. The objective is to fortify emotional resilience – to accept the emotional weight of the feedback without letting it dent your self-esteem. It calls for a unique blend of emotional acceptance and rational ignorance, especially towards aspects of feedback that might be non-constructive or irrelevant. The response here is one of gratitude, focusing on the supportive nature of the feedback while maintaining confidence in your abilities. It's about acknowledging the encouragement and selectively ignoring the non-constructive elements, ensuring they don't impede your self-assurance or professional trajectory.

Constructive Action: Navigating Between Emotional Rejection and Rational Analysis

Feedback Giver: The Critical Analyst

Envision a feedback scenario where the giver is a critical analyst, focusing sharply on areas needing improvement. Initially, this type of feedback might trigger an emotional rejection due to its directness or perceived severity. The art lies in transcending this emotional response, moving towards a rational and analytical perspective. This shift is essential for extracting actionable insights embedded within the criticism. The response involves a temporary suspension of emotional reactions to concentrate on the logical dimensions of the feedback. This methodical approach allows for pragmatic changes in your work, based on a rational interpretation of the critical analysis, despite the initial emotional discomfort.

Disengagement: The Intersection of Emotional Rejection and Rational Ignorance

Feedback Giver: The Disconnected Director

Finally, we encounter feedback that is often broad, high-level, and seemingly disconnected from specific, actionable objectives. This type emanates from the 'Disconnected Director,' whose feedback may lack direct relevance or constructiveness. The approach here is one of both emotional rejection and rational ignorance. It's about acknowledging the feedback with politeness and professionalism while consciously choosing not to integrate it into your action plans. The focus remains steadfast on your overarching professional goals and strategies, ensuring that this type of feedback does not derail or distract from your defined path.

Implementing the Matrix

Self-Awareness: Charting Your Feedback Response Journey

A pivotal step in applying this matrix in a professional context is the cultivation of self-awareness. This involves a deep, introspective understanding of your habitual responses to feedback. Are you quick to deflect criticism, or do you internalize it too deeply? The goal is to navigate towards a more balanced approach, where feedback is neither defensively rejected nor accepted without critical thought.

This journey of self-awareness requires honesty and vulnerability, as you assess and refine your reactions to feedback, ensuring they align more closely with the ideal approaches outlined in the matrix. It's about transforming feedback into a mirror, reflecting both your professional competencies and your ability to adapt and grow.

Interpersonal Skills: Adapting to the Feedback Giver's Style

Another crucial aspect is honing your interpersonal skills, specifically in terms of tailoring your responses to match the style of the feedback giver. This doesn't mean compromising your authenticity but rather adapting your approach to foster more effective communication.

For instance, with a 'Constructive Mentor', your response might be more open and collaborative, while with a 'Disconnected Director', it might be more about polite acknowledgment without deep engagement. This adaptive strategy enhances the quality of interactions, ensuring that the exchange is not just a one-way street but a dynamic dialogue that benefits both parties.

The overarching goal of this matrix is to harness feedback as a relentless tool for professional growth. This means viewing feedback, irrespective of its source or style, as an opportunity for continuous improvement. It's about developing a mindset that sees every piece of feedback as a stepping stone towards your professional betterment.

Whether it's a constructive critique from a mentor or a vague comment from a superior, each piece holds value. The key is to distill this value into actionable insights, using them to refine your skills, strategies, and professional demeanor. This relentless pursuit of growth through feedback is what ultimately defines a successful and adaptive professional journey. Whether contemplating a shift in roles, venturing into a new industry, or considering a strategic career pause, the insights gained from feedback play a significant role.

05

Precision in Action

The Operational Trinity: Order, Direction, and Delegation

The corporate jungle is something else. It's filled with dizzying highs and nervewracking lows, often reminding me of those childhood adventures through uncharted woods. The destination is always clear: that shining ray of success. Yet, the path to get there is a labyrinth of choices, each more daunting than the last. And while some folks get lost in the shuffle, others — the real masters— have a knack for cutting through the noise. Their focus lies in drawing clear lines, setting a distinct direction, and knowing when to take a step back.

Reflecting on my Bschool days, I recall Maya, an astute batchmate whose ambition was palpable during our countless caffeinefuelled discussions. While most of us were still grappling with market dynamics, she was the kind always two steps ahead, scribbling game plans on notepads. It was clear she was destined for big things. So when she landed a role at a topdog tech firm, none of us blinked an eye.However, the department she stepped into was far from structured—it was a maelstrom of hazy responsibilities and ambiguous deadlines.

Did she panic? No. Instead, Maya channeled the strategist in her. She went back to the drawing board, or in this case, to those Bschool frameworks we'd pored over, sometimes debated, during our study sessions. With a finetooth comb approach, she began the arduous task of delineating roles, setting clearcut boundaries, and establishing accountability. It wasn't just about telling people what to do, it was about showing them the bigger picture, their place in it, and the path to get there.

It wasn't just about restructuring, though. Maya's magic touch lay in her ability to instill a sense of purpose in her team. The department's transformation wasn't merely operational—it was cultural. By laying out clear boundaries, every team member now had a roadmap, a clearer understanding of their contributions to the bigger picture.

Maya's tale is more than just a Bschool success story. It hails the power of clarity in professional advancement. Whether you're in the early stages of your career, looking to leave your mark, or a seasoned leader aiming to steer the ship with assurance, the principle reigns: clear boundaries pave the path to consistent excellence.

Whenever I think of her journey, it's a stark reminder: In the corporate wilderness, it's not just about survival, but how you chart your path. And with the right compass, the world's your oyster.

Providing Direction Towards Common Goals for Career Ascension

In the pursuit of career ascension, having a comprehensive strategy is paramount. But more than just having a roadmap, it's about understanding the terrain, knowing where the pitfalls lie, and recognizing the shortcuts that can expedite the journey. This is the philosophy of channeling energies effectively towards a common career goal, and I found a tool that brings this perspective into sharp focus.

During an introspective period of my career, I sought insights from my peers. I requested them to submit a BAFA sheet, hoping to better understand how top performers navigated their daily operations. The results were eyeopening.

Understanding the BAFA Sheet

Link:https://docs.google.com/spreadsheets/d/1kX5NQLUzyVk-IYQ70oM47WSWPLpXOMf17_zfQenN6Ho/edit#gid=0

Bandwidth: This speaks to how one allocates their time, a clear reflection of priorities.

Actions: These are the initiatives taken, the tasks embraced, and the challenges tackled.

Frequency: This refers to a measure of consistency, this represents how often one revisits certain tasks or responsibilities.

Automation: Identifying areas where repetitive tasks can be automated, allowing more bandwidth for strategic endeavors.

The Statistical Unveiling

- A sizeable 20% of daily hours were being eaten up by meetings, many of which were not directly advancing individual career goals.
- 10% of routine activities had potential for automation, presenting opportunities for more strategic, careeradvancing initiatives.
- And only 5% genuinely required a mentor's or a superior's guidance for alignment with overarching career aspirations.
- The BAFA exercise shone light on a key aspect of career growth: It's not just about the hard work but smart work. Understanding where time and effort are spent can pinpoint areas where one can bring more value, increase visibility, and position oneself as indispensable.

For those looking to ascend, the lesson is clear: steer your own ship. This means taking control of your time, focusing on initiatives that matter, and seeking out tasks that align with larger career goals. The BAFA sheet, in this context, isn't just a tool but a compass, guiding professionals to calibrate their actions in a direction that ensures consistent upward mobility.

Delegating Effectively: Trusting and Empowering Teams for Optimal Results and Career Ascension

Imagine this: you've mapped out the terrain using the BAFA sheet, you're steering your ship towards your career goals, and the waters are getting rougher. Do you try to man every oar yourself or trust your crew to keep the ship sailing smoothly?

In the journey of career ascension, one of the most vital skills that separates potential leaders from the crowd is the art of effective delegation. It's not just about offloading tasks to lighten one's plate, it's about recognizing strengths, nurturing growth in others, and sculpting a team that amplifies overall productivity and innovation. It's in this collective effort that individual career progression truly finds its pace.

The Mathematics of Growth Through Delegation

A thought experiment— if one person, no matter how competent, attempts to do ten tasks, they can at best give 10% of their energy to each task. However, if these tasks were delegated to ten different individuals, each with a unique skill set apt for the task, the collective energy spent becomes 100% for each task. The result? Not just enhanced productivity, but a notable increase in the quality of output.

The Intangible Rewards of Delegation

While delegation offers tangible results in terms of efficiency, the intangible rewards are where career ascension truly accelerates. By delegating:

You create leaders: By giving team members ownership of tasks, you're fostering leadership skills in them. Today's delegate could be tomorrow's team leader, and your foresight in identifying and nurturing that potential can earmark you for senior leadership roles.

You develop a reputation as a team builder: Organizations value individuals who can build strong, effective teams. Such a reputation can open doors to roles involving larger team management, strategy, and planning.

You free up bandwidth for strategic thinking: While the team takes on the operational tasks, you have more time for bigpicture thinking, innovation, and strategic planning, all of which are invaluable for career advancement.

The Trust Factor in Delegation

Now, a pivotal aspect of delegation is trust. Delegating isn't merely assigning tasks it's about placing trust in team members, believing in their capabilities, and providing them the autonomy to approach challenges. This creates a positive feedback loop. When teams feel trusted, they not only rise to the occasion but also innovate, leading to outcomes that might surpass expectations.

Thus, the essence of delegation as a tool for career ascension lies in the understanding that career growth isn't a solitary journey. By uplifting and empowering those around us, we lay down a foundation for our own ascent. It's alike building a human pyramid the higher one wants to go, the stronger the base needs to be. And effective delegation is the cornerstone of that strong, elevating base.

Mastering Situational Strategy: Applying Murphy's Law

The TwoFold Classification

Regardless of whether one prioritizes plan A or leans towards plan B when faced with challenges, a foundational understanding is key: recognize what might cause a strategy to falter. At the heart of this lies Murphy's Law, which suggests that if something can go wrong, it will. For an emerging manager, dissecting situations into two primary categories as we discussed in the beginning- 'controllable' and 'uncontrollable' offers a clearer viewpoint and prepares them for the percentage of potential failures.

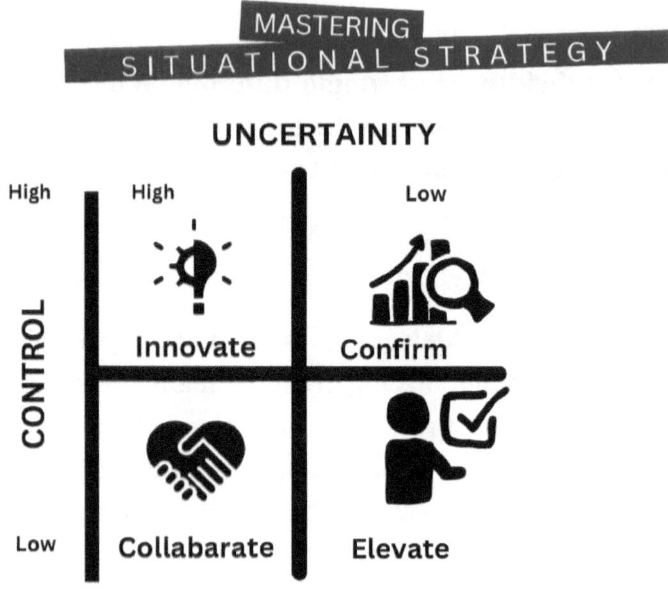

Conform

In landscapes of low uncertainty and limited controllability, the smart move is often to adhere to established protocols. By aligning with known methodologies and upholding organizational standards, you can ensure consistent and effective performance.

Collaborate

Venturing into territories with high uncertainty but restricted control demands collective intelligence. Pooling resources, sharing diverse perspectives, and forging strategic alliances can illuminate paths that were previously obscure, ensuring smoother navigation.

Elevate

Positioned in an arena where control is abundant but uncertainty is minimal, professionals have an avenue to truly shine. Rather than merely meeting expectations, the goal here is to surpass them — to not just play the game but to elevate it.

Innovate

Operating in a sphere with abundant control and glaring uncertainty offers an exciting challenge. Here, the conventional won't suffice. It's an open canvas, an invitation to experiment, disrupt, and introduce pioneering solutions that not only resolve the immediate challenge but also set new industry standards.

As we navigate through these varying landscapes of control and uncertainty, employing diverse strategic approaches, we are led to the crucial phase of execution. It's one thing to devise a strategy, but the true test lies in its execution.

That's where the ART of Execution – Accuracy, Responsiveness, Timeliness – finds its place.

The ART of Execution

While each term might ring a bell, together they create a pathway for success. As we unpack this, I want you to think of precision as a way of life rather than as a skill. Let's explore how to transform our work, one precise move at a time.

Accuracy: Ensuring Every Action Counts

When we are constantly pushed to move faster, it's tempting to let details slide. Yet, it's in these details that the magic truly happens. Each action we undertake, no matter how trivial it may seem, has a ripple effect on the outcomes we aim to achieve. It's this dedication to precision that differentiates a job done from a job well done.

Take a moment and recall the last time you truly immersed yourself in a task, ensuring every aspect was just right. That's the heart of pinpoint planning—making sure that every element aligns to create a successful outcome.

There are moments in our career that stand out, not for the praise or accolades, but for the tough lessons they teach us. I, too, have been through such treacherous phases, and it's during those trying times that I realized the true mettle of decisionmaking.

I vividly remember an episode from the early chapters of my professional narrative. With fire in my belly and dreams in my eyes, I was eager to establish myself as the linchpin, the one everyone could rely on. It's easy, in retrospect, to point fingers and say my superiors should have guided me better. But in all honesty, many of the mishaps wee because of my overeagerness combined with lackluster communication and premature execution.

As anyone climbing the corporate ladder would attest, managers have a panoramic view, but it's up to us to detail our little piece of that expansive picture accurately. The scenario took a dramatic turn when a distributor, who wasn't just another name on the list but contributed to a significant 20% of my region's revenue, faced financial turmoil. This jolted our welloiled FMCG distribution chain, where the regular inventory movement is like a beating heart, it was essential for survival. With the distributor's dip in performance, our numbers wobbled and it was as if the heart of our region had skipped a beat.

With passion often mistaken for haste, I took this issue to my superior, expecting guidance, perhaps even a solution. The advice was crisp : replace the distributor. Young and naive, I saw it as a directive and didn't pause to question or weigh its gravity. It was this blindspot, this enthusiasm without contemplation, that became my undoing. The complex relationships and dependencies in a smaller town like ours wasn't something I had factored in. The exit of a significant distributor without a backup plan in place wasn't just a hiccup.Indeed, it was an upheaval.

In the thick of it, two stressful months went by before I stumbled upon a distributor who truly understood the potential of our brand. Their financial stability was commendable, but it was their shared enthusiasm and forwardthinking vision that stood out. Looking back, that challenging phase was less about the hurdles and more about the learning.

If you're stepping into the professional space or even if you're kneedeep in it, here are some nuggets of wisdom I've gathered that can help you ensure accuracy in every action:

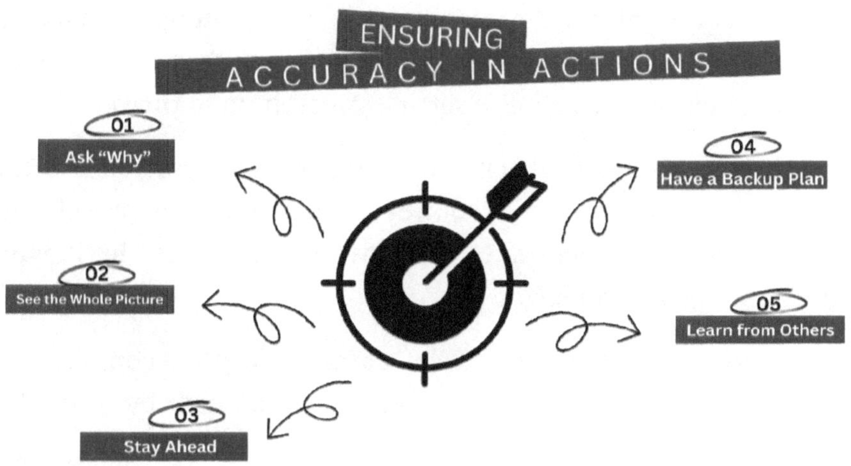

Ask "Why": It's simple. Whenever you're about to roll up your sleeves for a task, take a little pause. Seek the purpose behind it. Grasping the 'why' ensures that you move in the right direction and ties your actions to a broader objective.

See the Whole Picture: Decisions, even seemingly minor ones, can ripple out. Before you decide, envision the scenarios. Understand the possible aftermaths and be geared up for them.

Stay Ahead: Don't just react. Anticipate. Constantly look for alternatives and stay ready. This approach ensures you aren't just responding to events but shaping them.

Have a Backup Plan: Change is the only constant. This applies to the dynamic world of business. Regardless of your role, having an alternative plan in your back pocket can be a lifesaver.

Learn from Others: Connect with those who've been in the trenches. Absorb their tales of triumphs and missteps. Their experiences can guide you away from common pitfalls and towards tried and true methods.

The early stages of one's professional journey, although challenging, are filled with invaluable lessons. By embracing these challenges and absorbing their lessons, you're setting yourself up to thrive.

All of these lessons come back to our fundamental principle: Accuracy. Each step, each decision, requires a meticulous approach. After all, ensuring every action counts involves accuracy in judgment, understanding, and foresight.

As we delve deeper, another facet comes into play, complementing our accuracy. Enter Responsiveness—championed by the Kaizen Methodology.

Responsiveness The Kaizen Methodology

Being responsive is no longer just a commendable attribute in the corporate landscape—it's an imperative. It's about how promptly we align ourselves to evershifting dynamics, the depth of understanding with which we weather through unexpected disruptions, and the genuine poise we maintain when faced with the unexpected. It's this readiness and the ability to pivot that truly carves the path to success.

Reflecting on the distributor setback from earlier, the need to promptly replace such a pivotal piece of our revenue puzzle highlighted an important lesson. Speed is crucial, but what's equally important is the clarity of thought accompanying it. A quicker and more thoughtful response back then might have reduced the turbulence. Responsiveness, then, isn't just about rapid actions but also ensuring those actions are wellconsidered.

Being responsive is more than just a reactive approach, it's about foresight. It's the capability to anticipate, even if just slightly ahead of time. Consider the story of Netflix. They started as a DVD by mail service and could have easily been outmoded with the rise of digital streaming. But they responded proactively, pivoting their business model to online streaming way before most competitors caught on, effectively turning potential challenges into major strengths.

As it is widely noted, "Adapting to change is not about speed alone, but about depth, understanding, and foresight." In an industry like sales, it's easy to get caught up in the daily grind, always chasing the next big opportunity. The allure of charting fresh territories is tempting, but wisdom often lies in tracing back the steps of those who've walked before you. This notion became crystal clear to me early on in my journey with a leading Home and Health MNC.

When the baton of a significant sales role was passed to me, I was eager but also pragmatic. The legacy of my predecessor, a well respected figure, loomed large. But instead of letting that shadow intimidate me, I saw it as a treasure trove of knowledge. Before I could carve out my path, I knew I needed to understand his.

Upon reaching out, our conversation quickly turned to his passion projects, the initiatives that were close to his heart. His enthusiasm was palpable as he detailed his foray into the institutional market, a segment often termed as HORECA in FMCG lingo. My stationed city, a burgeoning hub for IT industries, was poised to be the next big playground for home cleaners. But the story didn't end there.

While absorbing his success stories was enlightening, I was more intrigued by the hurdles he faced. After all, it's often the missteps that provide the most profound insights. I pressed on, eager to know more about the strategies that didn't pan out. What were the initiatives that sounded great on paper but faltered in execution?

Taking a deep breath, I thought of 'Kaizen'. It's funny how some philosophies that were intially alien resonate deeply with you once you truly grasp their essence. Kaizen, a Japanese concept, means 'change for better'. But it's not about a monumental shift overnight. Rather, it's the dedication to those tiny, daybyday improvements, the ones that compound over time and make all the difference.

The wisdom in Kaizen reminded me that every change, however minute, shapes the outcome. So, drawing inspiration, I ventured forth. The trend was clear—there was a palpable shift from unbranded to branded products in the institutional market. I wasn't going to let this insight go untapped. Expanding our range to include air cleaners and tailored bathroom solutions, I tried to cater precisely to this segment's unique needs. But the twist in my strategy? Pairing a wellloved brand with an emerging one, offering them in a package deal. Add to that a tiered pricing model, and we were turning heads.

However, what truly set my strategy apart was my focus on the market's influencers—the big players. I knew that in sales, trust is often built on seeing tangible results. So, I aligned with the major traders, leveraging their trust to vouch for our product's worth. It was heartening to see that once they believed in our vision, many others followed suit.

Reflecting on this journey, I'm reminded of a simple yet profound quote: "In learning from the past, we carve a brighter future." This isn't just a catchy phrase. realworld examples reinforce its truth. Take LEGO, for instance. A brand that has brought joy to many, it faced a bleak horizon in the early 2000s. But instead of merely seeking new paths, they turned to their roots. They revisited their past, both the highs and the lows. By reengaging with their core audience and addressing past mistakes, LEGO rejuvenated its brand, reminding everyone of the timeless joy of building dreams, one block at a time.

This experience, intertwined with the principle of Kaizen, reaffirmed my belief in the power of continuous learning and improvement. Sometimes, the real impact is felt not through what we loudly declare, but through the subtle cues, our peers pick up from us. Let's now delve into the third part of the ART of Execution framework timeliness.

Timeliness: Clockwork Precision

Time is the silent narrator of our stories. It's not just about the ticking clock, but the moments between each tick, filled with decisions, actions, and pauses.

Imagine the quiet satisfaction of delivering a project not just on time, but with a finesse that makes everyone pause. It's about setting a standard. When we honor deadlines, we're saying, "I value your time as much as mine." It's a silent nod of mutual respect in hallways, meetings, and emails. In our careers, time isn't just chronological, it's emotional, filled with potential. A prompt decision can open doors, while delays might close them.

Much like the fabric of time, cities too have a rhythm every lane whispering a story of dreams and opportunities. One unassuming day, amidst the city's rhythm and the hum of twowheelers, I met Rajan. A spirited founder, he was the brainchild behind a budding startup that dared to dive into the complex sphere of two wheeler loan lending. Despite being just 24 months into the journey, they'd already tasted the ups and downs familiar to any startup narrative. And like many, they stood at an inflection point, pondering their next move.

Rajan shared their story. Their operations were layered with numerous human engagements.They would scout for twowheeler enthusiasts, gently nurture these initial sparks into genuine interest, and then embark on the detailed process of assessing loan eligibility. Then came the task of arranging test drives, ensuring diligent followups to clinch the deal, navigating the paperwork for loan approvals, and finally, the joy of handing over the keys. It was a rewarding, yet exhaustive journey.

The dilemma was how to refine this multifaceted process, reduce waiting times, and ensure every customer left with a smile.

Drawing from my engagements with various startups, a potential solution dawned. I proposed the MoSCoW method to Rajan as a way to bring structure and clarity to their operational challenges.

The MoSCoW Method: Turning Time into an Ally

For the uninitiated, the MoSCoW method might just seem like a clever wordplay, but it's far more than that. It breaks down into Must have, Should have, Could have, and Won't have, serving as a guiding force in the everevolving world of decisionmaking. By dividing tasks based on their urgency and importance, it ensures that priorities never get muddled.

Must Have: These elements sit at the heart of any project, the absolute essentials. For Rajan's startup, it became apparent that having a digitalized system to swiftly capture and closely monitor potential leads was imperative. Another gamechanger? An online system that would allow prospects to check their loan eligibility upfront. This not only promised a smoother customer journey but also ensured that the team didn't spend precious time on leads that wouldn't convert.

Should Have: These are enhancements that elevate the user journey, though they might not be as critical as the musthaves. Flexibility became our watchword here. We realized that giving prospects the autonomy to schedule test drives, and even better, offering them the convenience of home test drives, would amplify the customer experience. And with a team dedicated solely to relentless followup, the conversion rates were set to see an uptick.

Could Have: These are the cherries on top, delightful but not immediately essential. One such idea that bubbled up was a loyalty program for repeat customers or those bringing in referrals. As tempting as it was to roll this out, given the resources it demanded, we decided it would be a feather in our cap for a later date, post ironing out the kinks in the main processes.

Won't Have (at least for now): Every entrepreneur has a vision that stretches beyond the horizon. Rajan was no different. He was eager to branch out into insurance packages and aftersales services. But after some contemplation, we both agreed that these ventures, while promising, should wait. The focus needed to be on making the primary loanlending journey as fluid as possible first.

The Metric that Matters: "ValuetoTime" (VTT)

Now, reimagine this principle of Kaizen colliding with the world of metrics — those numeric reflections of our corporate dreams and nightmares. In the dizzying maelstrom of the corporate sphere, where every fleeting day introduces a new metric or measure, there arises a North Star to guide lost souls — the "ValuetoTime" (VTT) metric.

VTT isn't just another fleeting corporate buzzword. It's the embodiment of Kaizen in the realm of time management and productivity. By blending the ethos of continuous improvement with the pragmatic realities of everyday tasks, VTT shines a spotlight on efficiency. It becomes more than just a measure; it's a mantra. It nudges managers to look beyond the obvious, to delve deep into their processes, refining and sculpting them to perfection. Every minute, every action is weighed against its value, echoing the Kaizen spirit of making today better than yesterday.

Key Pillars of VTT

3 PILLARS OF VALUE TO TIME

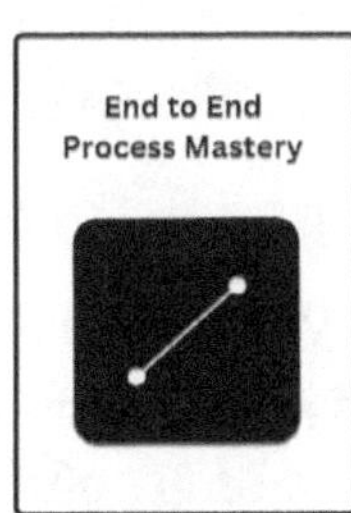

Foundations of ValuetoTime (VTT)

Streamlined Action Time: With VTT, every task is a testament to efficiency. As teams refine their approach, they save crucial hours, allowing them to shift focus to strategic initiatives that drive tangible progress.

Elevated Team Productivity: VTT shines a light on potential bottlenecks, paving the way for smoother operations and strengthened collaboration. By continuously seeking areas of improvement, managers harness their team's full potential, resulting in optimal productivity and unmatched outcomes.

EndtoEnd Process Mastery: Beyond isolated improvements, VTT champions a holistic approach to workflow enhancement. By identifying and addressing inefficiencies throughout the process, teams ensure maximum value delivery to both clients and stakeholders.

To all the visionaries managing teams: consider embracing "ValuetoTime" as your lodestar. Immerse in the philosophy of unending refinement, champion your team's ascent, and marvel as your collective efficiency reaches uncharted territories.

From Vision to Victory

While ambition drives the vision forward, it's the details and precision that often determine the trajectory of success. However, cutting corners isn't the answer. The art lies in optimizing processes while ensuring that quality remains uncompromised. It's about knowing where to invest time and resources, and where automation and system upgrades can save both. As we pave the path towards success, we understand that excellence is not a destination but a consistent practice.

It's fascinating how one decision, one change, or even one insight can spark a series of wins in business. Just like placing a single domino correctly can lead to a cascade, so can strategic moves in business lead to a ripple effect of accomplishments. And often, these achievements aren't just isolated victories; they feed into each other, creating momentum that propels the business forward. Understanding this interconnectedness, and acting with precision at pivotal moments, can redefine the trajectory of an organization's journey.

Drawing from such experiences, I've come to realize that our career trajectories aren't just measured by the height we achieve but by the pivots we dare to make. While ascending through career possibilities, sometimes it takes a Columbuslike spirit to journey through uncharted waters, seeking new horizons and opportunities.

The Columbus Framework

Ecommerce in 2014 was like a bustling bazaar, bursting with fresh energy and opportunities at every turn. Chennai, in particular, was a hub of activity with around 4050 new ecommerce platforms springing to life. Many businesses watched from the sidelines, uncertain of this new digital terrain. But a select few, like HUL, decided to dive in headfirst, tweaking their classic strategies—the 4 Ps—to fit this evolving landscape.

In the midst of this, I felt a spark of curiosity. There was a story unfolding, and I wanted to be part of it. As I connected with these freshfaced startups, a pattern began to emerge. There was untapped potential, especially in promoting larger Stock Keeping Units (SKUs), which hinted at a surge in sales waiting just around the corner. But it wasn't all smooth sailing. To truly harness this potential, I needed to get into the minds of the distributors—the heartbeat of the FMCG sector.

These distributors were cautious by nature. With profit margins as narrow as 46%, they operated with precision, ensuring every move was calculated to avoid bad debts. Gaining their trust and understanding their perspective was crucial. It became my mission to bridge the gap between the promise of ecommerce and the pragmatic approach of these distributors. And so, the Columbus Framework took shape, rooted in exploration, understanding, and collaboration.

In ecommerce, every handshake, every agreement, every unsent email carried the weight of human emotions: hopes, hesitations, and hardearned dreams. I remember being right in the middle of it, feeling the pulse of the industry, sensing both the eagerness and caution in the air.

The new ecommerce vendors, brighteyed and ambitious, were hunting for opportunities to set themselves apart. For them, bulk packs with tantalizing customer discounts were like gold. If there was an added bonus in the margins? Well, that was the cherry on top.

Meanwhile, the distributors, with their deeprooted experience and caution learned from years in the game, wanted surety. They valued prompt payments, smooth operations, and the assurance that their investments would bear fruit. They weren't looking for miracles, just consistent, reliable outcomes.

Seeing the contrasting desires, I introduced the auto PO system. It was simplicity at its best: a nononsense method streamlining the sales process for everyone. But I didn't stop there. By suggesting distributors highlight other brands they championed, I saw pathways open up for new business collaborations. Aligning distributors' routes with their plans? That was a gamechanger, bringing a rhythm to what was once chaotic.

The change was nothing short of incredible. What started as a modest contribution from ecommerce sales grew nearly from 0.05% to 7% in a mere three months. But beyond these numbers, it was the relationships built, the trust nurtured, and the collaborative spirit that made all the difference. Each decision, each pivot, echoed the heartbeat of the very humans that make up the industry.

With that in mind, let's dive into the nuances of career trajectories, which often mirror this kind of dynamic change.

The Career Ladder and the Precision Pivot

Ascending one's career isn't about following a straight, predefined path. It's about the decisions made at critical junctures, those moments of hesitation, contemplation, and eventual resolution. Sometimes, it's a subtle shift in focus, at other times, a complete change in direction, but always with a purpose.

Career crossroads are common. Everyone faces them. What differs is how we approach these intersections. Do we pause, deliberate, and take a measured step forward? Or do we rush, driven by external pressures, often missing the signposts that could guide us? The secret lies in recognizing these pivotal moments and making precise moves that align with our personal and professional goals.

Yet, no matter which direction we choose, our true value in the professional realm remains tethered to our execution.

Becoming Indispensable: Elevate Your Role through Execution Mastery

In the professional space, true value doesn't stem from how many hours you clock in or how often you're seen in meetings. It's about how you approach your tasks, the depth of understanding you bring, and the outcomes you produce.

To elevate your role is to dive deeper into your responsibilities, to understand the 'whys' behind the 'whats,' to look for solutions before problems even arise. It's about being that person others can rely on, not because you're always available, but because you bring clarity, efficiency, and a touch of brilliance to what you do.

What about titles? They're just labels. But making a difference, leaving an imprint through your work, and earning the respect of peers—that's where the real deal is.

While becoming indispensable takes dedication, having guiding principles can accelerate one's journey. For me, the Matthew Principle became that catalyst.

The Matthew Principle: A Catalyst for My Journey

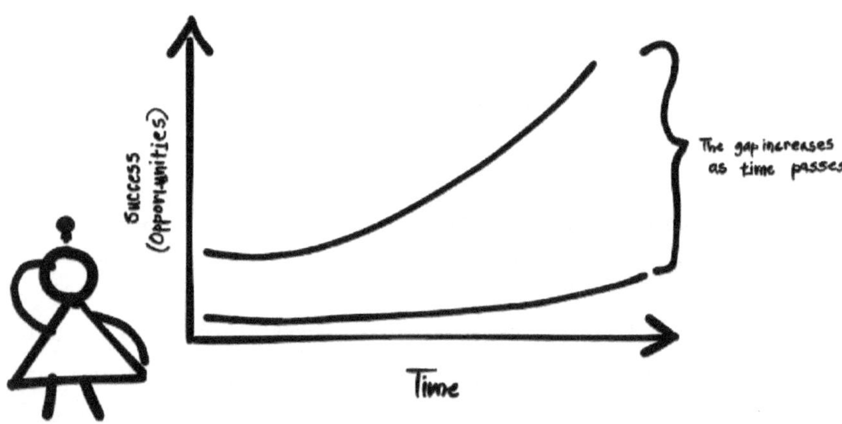

During the early phases of my career, I stumbled upon a guiding principle that resonated with my core: "To become the best, align yourself with the best." This wasn't just a catchy phrase for me. It bore the weight and clarity of the Matthew Effect, which essentially posits that advantages, once gained, tend to accumulate, while the lack of them can leave you trailing further behind.

But here's where it gets intriguing. The Matthew Effect isn't merely about gathering more; it's about the profound momentum one gains with each achievement. Think of it as a snowball effect; when you're ahead, every action, every decision, just propels you forward at an even greater pace. This insight ignited a clarity within me: if I aimed for unparalleled excellence, I needed to be amidst those who wouldn't settle for anything less than the best.

And so, my journey began. From joining forces with Colgate, the stalwarts of oral care, to collaborating with Reckitt, the undisputed champs of home care. From diving into the vast, dynamic world of Amazon to joining hands with Meesho, a revolutionary in social commerce, my career evolved into a series of deliberate choices. It wasn't about flaunting big brand names, but about immersing myself in ecosystems brimming with brilliant minds, where every day was a deep dive into learning, where challenges were embraced with gusto, and opportunities were just waiting to be seized.

Every role I stepped into was more than a task—it was a chance to redefine standards. The goals were always high, sometimes feeling just out of reach, but it was this remarkable stretch for the exceptional that helped me grow and evolve. You see, when you're constantly reaching for the stars, even the moon feels like just another pit stop.

I will admit that the journey wasn't always smooth, but the outcomes were undeniably rewarding. Every experience with the industry's frontrunners didn't just add to my resume, it etched into my professional identity, creating a narrative not many could claim. Working alongside these giants became a part of who I was, shaping my perspective and approach.

The Matthew Effect isn't just some highbrow theory to me. It's been the incredible ripple effect of one good choice leading to another. By embracing excellence and associating with the best, I didn't just progress, I thrived. And looking back, I cherish every choice, every turn, for they've made this journey not just successful, but truly memorable.

These affiliations soon became my unique selling point, turning the spotlight on me in a crowded room. And as doors of opportunities swung open, the allure of entrepreneurship beckoned. With these insights and experiences, I plunged into the world of startups, meeting challenges with fresh eyes yet seasoned judgment.

Drawing from these experiences, I began to discern patterns and derive personal strategies that would come to define my approach to professional growth. Eventually, I found my own mantra: the Work Role +1. It's closely similar to standing on your tiptoes, trying to glimpse the festivities of the next big carnival just around the corner.

I vividly recall a day early in my journey when this entire concept came to life. Walking beside a seasoned leader during a market visit, I anticipated a typical routine: a touchbase, a nod to how business was faring, perhaps a few shared anecdotes. But this outing took an unexpected turn.

When someone asks for our feedback, don't we often focus on the glitches rather than the highlights? It's a common tendency many of us have. But that day, the leader took a different approach. Instead of the usual "How's everything?", he asked with genuine curiosity, "How can we collaborate to boost your profits?" The dynamics changed instantly. It felt like we were partners in a startup, brainstorming the next innovative feature.

What genuinely took me by surprise, though, was the depth of his groundwork. He had sifted through mountains of data, pinpointing opportunities and gaps like a detective connecting the dots. By the time we started discussing, he was already a step ahead of being informed, he was charting the way forward. And in that moment, it dawned on me: to truly shine,you need to understand the entire narrative, being ready to adapt, and perhaps even pen the next chapter.

His genuine understanding of ROI, essential to every business, was truly captivating. Instead of throwing out broad ideas, he dived deep. Tweaking route plans, suggesting crosstraining opportunities for the team, and refining inventory management—his advice was detailed, targeted, and incredibly actionable. I could see the distributor, who started the day with evident reservations, slowly getting swayed by this refreshing mix of clarity and care. Even months after that day, people would bring up how enlightening that discussion had been, crediting the leader's insight and personable approach.

That day did more for me than years might have. It dawned upon me that real success doesn't come from just doing your job, but from expanding your vision beyond it. It's not merely about completing tasks, it's about understanding where they fit in the grander scheme of things.

This realization transformed my interactions, especially with vendors. Gone were the days of mere transactional talks; now, it was all about mutual growth and shared visions. Even a simple shift in my questions, like asking, "How can I support you to elevate your business?" led to richer, more meaningful conversations.

The Work Role +1 concept became about anticipating what comes next in your job. It's a broader perspective, a way to foresee challenges, and most crucially, a means to nurture relationships that thrive on mutual trust and ambition.

06

The Digital Imperative in Career Growth

Do you remember the first time you held a smartphone? The curious mix of excitement and awe as you swiped through apps, realizing that the world was literally at your fingertips? The transition wasn't just technological, it was emotional. Fast forward to today. The soft hum of a machine, an algorithm crunching vast data sets and the silent pulse of AI integrating into every facet of our lives—this isn't the world of tomorrow, it's today's pressing reality.

Imagine waking up to this world where machines predict our needs even before we voice them where they play the songs we're in the mood for or order our favorite meal when we've had a hard day. Sounds magical, doesn't it? But with this magic comes an urgent nudge, a whisper that tells us that staying afloat isn't enough anymore. As roles blur and adapt in this AIdriven epoch, one thing is crystal clear: To lead is to innovate.

Let's let the numbers talk for a moment. The World Economic Forum, in one of its recent articles, underscored the rapid and vast shift towards digital platforms. In just a few pivotal months, it's as if we've leaped half a decade into the future in our journey of consumer and business digital adoption. The onset of the global pandemic wasn't merely a health calamity, it served as a potent catalyst that urged even industries rooted in tradition to pivot toward the digital space.

Such brisk metamorphosis is, unsurprisingly, accompanied by its set of hurdles. Delving into a Gartner report, we uncover a telling narrative: a whopping 87% of senior business magnates affirm digitalization as a linchpin of their strategy. Yet, merely a handful seem truly prepared with the requisite skillset and roadmap to tread this fresh digital landscape adeptly. This discernible chasm isn't solely an organizational predicament but resonates as a loud and clear summon to individuals. It's an invitation, if you will, to enhance one's skill, to evolve and to seize control.

How do we ensure that amid all the algorithms and data, the heartbeats and human stories remain paramount? The key lies feeling the pulse, urgency, promise and the challenges of the digitalfirst approach. After all, the future isn't just something we enter, it's something we create.

You see, technology, with all its allure and promise, isn't the elixir that cures all our modern woes. Instead, imagine it as an adept enabler and a masterful instrument that, when handled with finesse, can fling open the gates to untold prospects.This is where a philosophy I hold dear comes into play, an idea I've dubbed as the "Trend + 1" approach.

Quick flashback to 2013. The buzz around digital marketing was just beginning. People were shifting from chalkandtalk to clickandlearn and I decided to be part of that wave. It was different, no doubt. The warmth of facetoface interactions was swapped for the cool glow of a computer screen. But the promise of learning something groundbreaking was too good to pass up.

This switch made all the difference when I joined Prione which soon became a part of Amazon India. Combining my new digital knowhow with my core sales skills felt like having a secret weapon. I was doing more than just understanding how Amazon's advertising worked, I was diving deep into the tiny details like how keyword searches functioned on the platform. It felt like peeking behind the curtain, understanding more than just the act but the entire show.

One day, driven by sheer curiosity, I started a little experiment. I wanted to know what items people frequently searched for on Amazon. While it wasn't technically part of my sales role, I've always believed in taking that extra step—the "+1 Approach." And boy, did it pay off. We found a trend: people were often looking up crafts and DIY projects. They clicked a lot but didn't add items to their carts. It seemed they were interested but something held them back.

Spotting this gap, we jumped in. We curated products that matched these search trends. The response was overwhelming. Clicks turned into carts and carts turned into confirmed orders. I meticulously documented this success and presented it to the higherups, showing them what was possible with a little outofthebox thinking.

The results were so impressive that our project expanded, adapting to different categories and becoming more strategic with each step. This journey, which began with a blend of newage skills and a proactive attitude, led to me clinching the "Cowboy Award."

The Role of Technological Acumen in DecisionMaking and Future Planning

We're living in an era where the term 'tech' prefixes everything, making the word as omnipresent as the technology it represents. When we sift through the techtalk, the reality becomes evident: in the current professional ecosystem, a deep grasp of technology isn't just advantageous—it's essential.

PwC's illuminating survey underscores this urgency: a staggering 77% of global CEOs pinpoint a deficiency in digital skills as the main hurdle in their path to innovation. Now, flip the coin. What if you're in that niche 23% that possesses these skills? Your value just skyrocketed.

So, what does this mean for the everyday professional? Let's delve deeper:

Decoding Decisionmaking with Tech: The line between tech and nontech roles blurs by the day. Whether you're strategizing a marketing campaign or driving HR initiatives, decisions are no longer made in boardrooms over coffee. They're made behind screens, powered by bytes of data. Drawing from the Deloitte Insights report, it becomes evident that businesses anchored in datadriven decisions don't just survive, they thrive. These companies boast a staggering 23fold increase in customer acquisition. Technological acumen is about delving into these data layers, interpreting patterns, anticipating trends and crafting strategies that align with these insights. It's not enough to skim the surface. Today's professional must dive deep, exploring the myriad intersections where technology meets business.

When one combines these insights with strategic action, the results can be transformative. As the boundaries of what technology can achieve expand, those equipped with the right skills will be at the helm, steering their organizations and their careers into territories of success.

Futureproofing with Foresight: We all recall the tales of Blockbuster and Kodak, industry titans that once stood tall but ultimately crumbled, unable to decode the writing on the digital wall. It's not just about the failure to adopt technology but the inability to foresee its transformative implications. As of 2022, big data analytics was integral to the operations of 85% of companies. The objective isn't merely to integrate new tools but to grasp the expansive ripple effects these tools can have on industries. Professionals who can perceive these nuances and understand the larger picture position themselves as key pillars within their organizations.

Personal Career Arc: If we step away from organizational charts and look at individual trajectories, technological acumen emerges as a defining catalyst. A whopping 92% of recruitment experts consider soft skills as pivotal as, if not more than, technical prowess. Here's the nuanced detail: within the umbrella of 'soft skills' today, digital literacy is prominent. While attributes like emotional intelligence and collaborative spirit are undeniably important, maneuvering through the digital space with finesse is becoming an imperative. The modern professional's toolkit should, therefore, house both the empathetic touch and the digital dexterity.

Drawing a parallel from the essence of adaptability discussed above, I would like to delve into an approach that I go back to: "Presentation + 1". With this approach, I've come to recognize an essential truth: brilliance in isolation has limited impact, but when paired with compelling presentation, its influence becomes boundless.

Circling back to 2017, a time when the buzz around data analytics was crescendoing, my journey took a significant turn. I opted to deep dive into an analytics course. Rather than simply hopping onto the trend bandwagon, I was guided by a vision — discerning the monumental role technology would soon command in steering decisions. Journeying through the intricate alleys of tools like SQL was enlightening, allowing me to weave through layers of data. However, it was Tableau that offered a canvas to paint these data points into cohesive, striking narratives.

With Tableau, I found myself in possession of a wand that could morph intricate datasets into visuals that spoke, resonated and lingered. Beyond the technological prowess, it nudged me towards the finesse of storytelling. Because data, when narrated effectively, turns into a compelling tale, wielding the might to sway opinions, reshape perspectives and ignite inspirations. And, I aimed to be that raconteur.

In boardrooms and team huddles, while many clung to their safety nets of conventional charts and dry spreadsheets, my presentations came alive with vibrant data landscapes. It was more than a display of my technological adeptness. It underscored my vision of the future. My data illustrations were no longer mere presentations, they metamorphosed into experiences, ensnaring attention, sparking curiosity and driving informed conclusions.

Yet, the true validation of my pioneering spirit wasn't confined to the applause or the appreciative glances exchanged during these sessions. The genuine acknowledgment surfaced when peers, both rookies and veterans, sought my insights, eager to unravel the magic of these newage tools. Sensing a window to sow the seeds of a culture steeped in perpetual evolution, I gladly donned the hat of a mentor.

Sharing became more than an act, it transformed into a responsibility, fortifying ties of trust, collaboration and mutual respect. While being hailed as techadept was rewarding, being the lighthouse guiding others was infinitely more gratifying.

The technical edge I honed empowered me, not solely through the arsenal of knowledge it furnished but through the avenues it opened for impactful communication and fostering growth. Today's era underscores the fact that possessing information is just half the battle won. The true triumph lies in how you package it, disseminate it and empower others with it.

Breaking Barriers and Thinking Beyond

Stagnation is the enemy of progress in a world dominated by rapid technological advancements and constant shifts in business paradigms. The key to career evolution lies not just in meeting the expectations set for us, but in challenging them, questioning them and at times, going beyond them. This is where the power of breaking barriers comes into play.

But what is the anatomy of a barrier?

More often than not, these barriers are psychological constructs. They might be borne from an industry's reluctance to change due to vested interests or from individual's innate apprehensions about treading unfamiliar paths. They can be the hesitations we feel due to ageold industry 'best practices' or the selfimposed limitations arising from doubts about our capabilities.

Remember, every industry disruptor or leading innovator we admire today didn't reach their pinnacle by adhering strictly to the rule book. They tinkered, tested and sometimes tore the rule book apart to script their own success story. If we aim to etch our mark and ascend in our careers, we must adopt this experimental mindset but with a calculated approach. Think of it as controlled chaos – where innovation is encouraged but every move is backed by research, analysis and an underlying strategy.

In the quest to break barriers and think beyond, initiating a change is only the first step. A change's true mettle is tested when it challenges deeprooted conventions. At such junctures, it's imperative to understand that simply identifying a need for change isn't the endgame. To truly surpass these barriers, one must gauge inherent apprehensions, confront them proactively and unite everyone under a shared vision.

Central to my professional ethos is the "Behaviour + 1" approach. It signifies that effecting change, especially when it vehemently defies entrenched norms, necessitates an added effort—an extra push or a '+1' to make it a reality.

Take, for instance, the onset of the smartphone revolution in the early 2010s. It heralded a significant shift for FMCG companies, signaling a transition from the traditional pen and paper to stateoftheart digital devices for sales operations. This ambition was trailblazing but like any revolutionary idea, it was met with its share of skeptics.

Talks of digitizing sales through "Palm tops" resonated in corporate corridors. The leadership envisioned a digitized future yet the ground teams approached it with caution. Their reservations reflected natural human hesitations: a seismic shift in daily operations, teething technological issues and a deepseated aversion to abrupt change.

Undeterred by these challenges, I sought to redefine my approach. Borrowing insights from Ohm's Law, I aimed to strategically tackle these resistance points. The challenges were twopronged: People and Process.

In the sphere of process management, I collaborated closely with project managers to ensure a smooth digital transition. However, while processes are malleable, altering human behavior proved more formidable.

Drawing parallels from Paytm and Google Pay's engagement models, I realized the transformative power of incentives. Could enticing rewards drive our sales team towards digital acceptance?

To effect this behavioral transition, I introduced the "3 Rs of Change": Rewards, Recognition, and Remuneration. My sway over remuneration was limited but rewards and recognition were tools I could deftly wield. I rolled out a pilot program, selecting a team of motivated sales professionals to experience the digital shift firsthand. As anticipated, we faced hiccups, but this trial was pivotal.

Following this intensive 45day phase, the outcome was revolutionary. We saw an unprecedented surge in productivity and my region took the lead, boasting a complete embrace of the digital sales framework.

In reflection, this journey was enlightening. It emphasized the need for understanding, unwavering determination and the impact of the "Behaviour + 1" methodology. More than just heralding change, it's about recognizing underlying concerns, addressing them decisively and fostering a unified drive towards a common goal. Though such endeavors present challenges, when approached with resolve, the resultant rewards, both tangible and intangible, are immensely gratifying.

The Adobe Paradigm: Fostering Innovation at Its Core

Amidst the myriad stories of successful transitions and transformations in the corporate realm, Adobe's metamorphosis stands as a paragon. This shift was not solely due to the advent of digital technology, but largely to the visionary leadership of Shantanu Narayen.

Under Narayen's stewardship, Adobe transcended its initial identity as a software developer and morphed into a vanguard of digital creativity and innovation. But how did Narayen cultivate such an atmosphere of relentless innovation at Adobe?

From the outset, Narayen comprehended that for Adobe to thrive in a fastevolving digital landscape, innovation couldn't merely be an afterthought—it had to be the organization's lifeblood. Rather than being content with Adobe's legacy products, he fostered a culture that perpetually asked, "What's next?" This perspective spurred teams to consistently push boundaries, ensuring Adobe was always a step ahead in the digital realm.

Beyond just championing innovation, Narayen believed in creating an ecosystem that was inherently geared towards avantgarde approaches. He recognized that innovation wasn't just about new products, it was equally about processes, customer engagement and fostering an internal environment where ideas could sprout and flourish.

To achieve this, Narayen implemented a dualpronged strategy. First, he ensured that the company's infrastructure was robust and agile, capable of swiftly pivoting to embrace emergent technologies. Secondly, he prioritized talent acquisition and development, focusing on onboarding individuals who were not just skilled but also possessed an innovative mindset.

His playbook didn't stop there. Narayen encouraged open dialogue, creating platforms where teams across hierarchies could share ideas, challenge norms and cocreate solutions. This democratization of idea generation ensured that innovation was not confined to a select few but was a collective pursuit.

Integrating the CEO Mindset into Daily Operations: Narayen's Blueprint for Career Ascension in the TechDriven Era

Shantanu Narayen's leadership at Adobe has stood as a beacon for professionals aiming to elevate their careers in the tech landscape. Narayen's blueprint vital lessons for individuals keen on adopting a CEO mindset. Drawing from the essence of our previous discussions, let's distill Narayen's strategies for career advancement in the digital age.

Visionary Planning with the Trend +1 Insight

A CEO is not just a decisionmaker but a visionary. Narayen has always emphasized looking beyond current market trends, resonating with our "Trend +1" approach. While the tech world marveled at software innovations, he foresaw the shift towards cloudbased solutions, positioning Adobe at the forefront of this transition. For individuals, this means not just mastering current tech skills but anticipating the next wave and preparing for it.

Operational Excellence and the Behaviour +1 Philosophy

Narayen's operational brilliance is rooted in his belief that good is not enough, one must strive for exceptional. This aligns perfectly with our "Behaviour +1" approach. He instilled a culture where teams not only met their targets but constantly sought ways to surpass them. In career ascension, it teaches professionals to consistently push their boundaries, aiming not just for competence but excellence.

Articulating Vision with the Presentation +1 Strategy

Narayen has been a master communicator, ensuring Adobe's mission and values were clear and compelling. Drawing parallels with our "Presentation +1" approach, he underlined the importance of not just having a vision but articulating it effectively. For tech professionals, this underscores the necessity of honing soft skills alongside technical expertise, ensuring they can convey their ideas persuasively in a collaborative environment.

Embracing Continuous Learning

In the techdriven era, the only constant is change. Narayen championed a culture of continuous learning at Adobe. He encouraged employees to regularly upskill, tapping into emerging technologies and methodologies. For career ascension, this approach is invaluable.

It teaches professionals to remain perpetual students, always staying ahead of the learning curve.

Building Collaborative Ecosystems

Narayen understood the tech world's interconnected nature. Under his leadership, Adobe forged partnerships, integrated acquisitions seamlessly, and built a collaborative ecosystem. For individuals, this strategy translates to the importance of networking and fostering collaborative relationships in the tech domain, ensuring they're always plugged into opportunities and innovations.

As we circle back to the heart of this chapter, one message stands out: Digital isn't just a facet of modern career growth—it's the backbone. From understanding the pulse of technological innovation to incorporating a digitalfirst approach in our professional pursuits, the digital imperative is undeniable.

07

The Path to Prosperity

Finance, at first glance, may seem like a space dominated by cold numbers. Yet, when we begin to peel back its layers, we realize it is far more. Mastering the language of finance is imperative. It should not be regarded merely as an auxiliary skill but rather as a fundamental tool for rapid career advancement.

Grappling with the complexities of the financial terrain is a cornerstone of judicious decisionmaking. It transforms the process from an intuitive gamble to a strategic choice informed by economic foresight and thorough market intelligence. It's about applying a discerning eye to the potential gains of your endeavors, guaranteeing that they augment the financial health of your company and chart a rising course for your career.

A nuanced grasp of finance equips you to uncover avenues for cost containment and the enhancement of operational efficiencies. This venture goes beyond mere fiscal pruning, it's an intelligent redistribution of assets to ventures ripe with promise for robust rewards—a boon for both the enterprise and your own marketability within your field.

Financial acumen pushes you to think critically about investment—in technology, in systems, in people—and the timing of these investments. It urges you to question: Is this the right moment to push for a new project? How will the expected returns on this investment elevate my position within the company? This sense of urgency is crucial, as timing can be the difference between a career leap and a stagnant trajectory.

Furthermore, financial literacy extends your vision beyond the immediate horizon to encompass the broader vista of your company's position within the wider market. It involves decoding economic patterns, adapting to regulatory shifts, and staying attuned to international fiscal trends that bear the weight to reshape your industry. Such deepseated awareness earmarks you as a professional with a progressive mindset, one poised to steer strategic maneuvers in tune with the prevailing financial winds.

In managing risks, my financial education was invaluable. It allowed me to predict downturns and plan accordingly. This proactive approach has been crucial, it was never about shying away from risks but about being prepared for them. This attitude has shown my superiors that my approach to growth is not just driven by ambition but is anchored in reality.

Those who command financial prowess steer their careers with authority. They are the ones who can argue for their initiatives, defend their budgets, and align their professional goals with the economic objectives of their employers. They're the professionals who don't just survive organizational reshuffles, they thrive in them, often emerging with their career paths accelerated.

Building upon our earlier discussion about the urgency of financial literacy in career development, let's delve into a critical aspect of this skill set – frugality.

Being the Frugal +1

To ascend to leadership, one must embody the principle of prudence in financial decisions. It's easy to misconstrue finance as a distant entity, disconnected from the daytoday responsibilities of most roles but this is a perilous misconception. Finance is not confined merely to the accounting department, it permeates every aspect of a business, influencing decisions across all levels and departments.

Take, for example, the crucial moment during my second year in a leadership role. A juncture arrived that tested my hiring strategies and my financial judgment. The decision at hand was whether to retain a senior resource who, despite their years of experience, was faltering in performance and discipline. Until that point, my recruitment experience was limited to individuals with 13 years of experience, and the prospect of hiring more seasoned professionals was uncharted territory for me.

In that moment of decisionmaking, I could have followed the beaten path, seeking out another seasoned professional to fill the shoes left vacant. But I chose a different route, driven by the instinct to bring in fresh energy and perspective rather than relying solely on years of experience. My attention turned to a vibrant salesperson from a lesserknown town in the TN coastal districts. He brought to the table enthusiasm and an entrepreneurial zeal that was hard to ignore. Recognizing the potential for growth and innovation, I ventured to bring him on board as a Sales Representative for the rural territories under my purview.

Presenting this unconventional choice to my manager was a challenge. Yet, the key lies in articulating the decision through the lens of financial prudence. By focusing on the economics – the stark fact that this candidate would cost a mere fraction of a more experienced hire – I spoke in a way that resonated with the management. The approval came swiftly, with minimal resistance, a testament to the persuasive power of a wellreasoned financial argument.

Disclaimer on Frugality

However, it's essential to clarify that frugality isn't about sheer costcutting. It's a nuanced practice of maximizing value per expenditure, of making informed choices that prioritize efficiency, sustainability, and impactful outcomes. In the business world, frugality is about stewardship of resources, exercising discretion, and fostering an environment where each investment is scrutinized for its potential return.

Companies treasure this frugal mindset not for the simple allure of savings but for the strategic advantage of sustainable, efficient growth. A professional who can stretch a dollar, not by diminishing quality or outcomes but by smart allocation and prioritization, becomes an invaluable asset. They signal to the company a capability to produce results while preserving, even augmenting, the organization's financial health.

This ethos of frugality, aligned with a commitment to performance, became a cornerstone of my approach to financial management within my role. Every choice presented an opportunity to question and innovate on how we could enhance efficiency without sacrificing quality. It was a constant balancing act, one that kept the profitability and health of the business at the forefront.

Strategic Financial Planning: Aligning Monetary Decisions with Career Objectives

Strategic financial planning within the context of career growth necessitates a convergence of practical financial management and targeted professional development. This sophisticated blend requires a step away from generalities and into tailored, actionable strategies that address the nuanced interplay between fiscal health and career progression. It is an ongoing process of calibrating your financial compass to the milestones on your career path.

To crystalize this concept, let's examine the trajectories of two corporate mavens whose fiscal strategies were instrumental in their ascent to the zenith of their careers. First, consider the journey of Indra Nooyi, the former CEO of PepsiCo. Her strategic financial acumen was evident in the company's revenue growth and in her personal career development. Nooyi masterminded investments in healthy product lines ahead of market trends, showcasing a prescient understanding of both financial foresight and consumer shifts. This in turn catapulted the company's profits and cemented her reputation as a visionary leader.

Then, there's the story of Anne Mulcahy, who took the helm of Xerox during a tumultuous period. Faced with the daunting task of steering a sinking ship, Mulcahy's financial savvy was critical. She didn't just slash costs, she scrutinized every line item to understand its impact on the business's health and growth potential. Her strategic decisions, such as the choice to invest in technology and customer service, reflected a deeper understanding of how financial choices could be leveraged to resuscitate and elevate a faltering company. Under her stewardship, Xerox underwent a remarkable transformation, turning from nearly bankrupt to profitable, and Mulcahy's role as a financially astute leader was undeniably at the core.

Drawing inspiration from Nooyi and Mulcahy, one sees that strategic financial planning is less about hoarding resources and more about intelligently allocating them toward opportunities that offer exponential career value. It's about investing in skills and education that will yield dividends in the form of promotions and leadership opportunities. It's about knowing when to tighten the fiscal belt to weather economic downturns and when to capitalize on financial surpluses to pursue growth ventures.

To forge a financial plan with career objectives at its core, professionals must start by scrutinizing their career landscape with a financier's eye. Where are the investments, the risks, and the potential returns in terms of career capital? They must dissect their professional goals as a financial analyst would examine an investment portfolio, assessing risks, timeframes, and expected outcomes.

Next, it's imperative to construct a budget that reflects this strategic career plan. Allocate resources not just based on current needs but future aspirations. This might mean setting aside funds for a specialized certification that can open doors to executive roles or earmarking savings for a startup venture that could catapult your career into entrepreneurship.

When it comes to risk anticipation, it's about identifying potential career hazards—such as industry volatility or technological obsolescence—and mitigating them with financial cushions that can fund transitions or education to pivot seamlessly into emerging domains.

Creating Contingency Plans: The Safety Nets of Career Progression

Contingency plans act as the strategic underpinning that allows professionals to navigate uncertainties with confidence in the highstakes arena of career progression. They serve as safety nets, carefully woven with the threads of foresight, flexibility, and meticulous preparation. The construction of these plans is not a mere exercise in pessimism, it is a proactive, bold acknowledgment that the path to the top is often unpaved and unpredictable. It is here, in the drafting of these plans, where urgency meets prudence, and gripping reality aligns with visionary foresight.

To create a solid contingency plan, we delve beyond standard riskaversion tactics, instead crafting a framework that is as dynamic as the careers it aims to protect. This framework rests on three pillars: anticipation, diversification, and transformation.

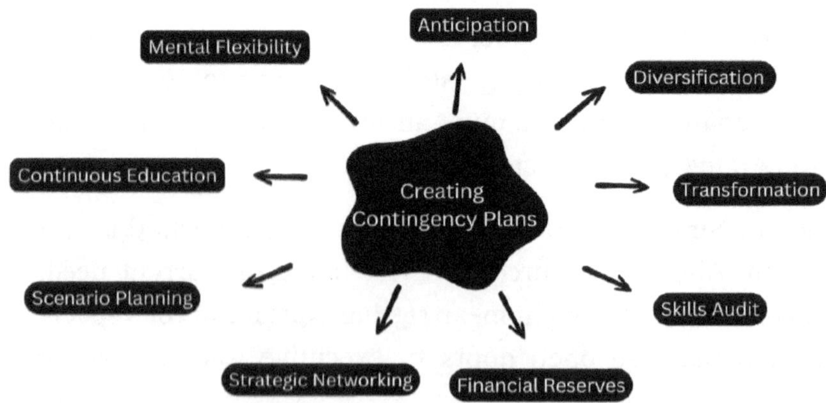

Anticipation: Reading the Wind

At the outset, professionals must cultivate the ability to anticipate potential career disruptors. This is not about gazing into a crystal ball, this involves honing a keen sense of industry trends, economic indicators, and technological advancements. One must learn to read the subtle shifts in market winds, interpreting the ripples before they become waves. This requires a commitment to continuous learning and an investment in a network of informants—mentors, colleagues, and industry groups—that can offer early warnings of impending changes.

Diversification: Not All Eggs in One Basket

The second pillar is diversification, a concept borrowed from finance but equally pertinent to career planning. Here, one's skillset, experience, and professional engagements must be spread across a spectrum of roles, industries, or disciplines. This diversification ensures that if one area faces a downturn, another can offer stability or even growth. It's about having a multifaceted profile, where being an expert in one field is complemented by being competent in several others.

Transformation: The Art of Pivoting

The final pillar, transformation, speaks to the ability to pivot. When faced with a roadblock, a career that has been strategically managed should be able to shift direction without losing momentum. This requires a mindset of adaptability and a professional identity that is versatile.

Implementing the pillars of a robust contingency plan translates into a series of strategic actions. Each step is both a line of defense and a launchpad for future growth.

Skills Audit: Mastery in Motion

A skills audit is a rigorous process that demands introspection and honesty. It's about laying all your professional cards on the table and seeing how they play against the everevolving game of industry demands. It requires one to be a student of the market, keenly aware of emerging technologies and shifting paradigms. For example, a software engineer might find their expertise in a legacy coding language diminishing in value. They must pivot, perhaps embracing the burgeoning field of machine learning, thus realigning their trajectory with the technological zeitgeist.

Financial Reserves: The Professional War Chest

Financial resilience cannot be overstated. The ability to weather a storm often hinges on the readiness of one's reserves. It's similar to the practice of prudent companies who allocate funds for research and development, not knowing which project will soar but understanding that investment is crucial for innovation. Similarly, professionals might channel a portion of their income into investments or side hustles.

Strategic Networking: The Coalition of Progress

Networking is the strategic alliance of mutual progress. It's forging connections that are symbiotic, where knowledge, opportunities, and support flow freely. A finance manager, for example, might connect with startup founders, other finance professionals, and software developers, creating a rich network of contacts that can open doors to new opportunities or offer insights that might pivot a career.

Scenario Planning: Charting the WhatIfs

Scenario planning is the professional equivalent of chess—it's about thinking several moves ahead. It's crafting a playbook for various career turns before they occur. A project manager might envision scenarios ranging from a promotion to the dissolution of their team. For each situation, they plot tactical responses, whether it's upskilling for the new role or preparing a portfolio to present to potential employers.

Continuous Education: The Knowledge Currency

In a world where knowledge is currency, continuous education is an investment in one's market value. This could manifest in a marketing professional obtaining a certification in digital analytics or an engineer learning project management to broaden their operational capabilities. These efforts compound over time, positioning the individual for a career that is sustainable and expansive.

Mental Flexibility: The Agile Mind

Embracing projects outside one's comfort zone fosters an agile mind. It's about being willing to pilot a new departmental initiative or volunteering for a crossfunctional project team. This adaptability was exemplified by a sales director who transitioned to leading a product innovation team, leveraging his clientfacing insights to drive new product development.

These steps, when implemented with commitment and strategic foresight, equip you with a robust framework to pivot with precision in the face of career uncertainties.

Warren Buffett From Simple Beginnings to Financial Maestro

In building strategic financial acumen, few narratives are as compelling and instructive as that of Warren Buffett. Buffett's journey from a paperboy in Omaha to the oracle of global finance is a masterclass in strategic financial principles, which when applied to career progression, can be transformative.

Foundations of Buffett's Approach

Value Investing as a Career Philosophy: Buffett's philosophy of value investing is more than a financial strategy; it's a professional ethos. Seek roles and projects that are undervalued those that offer more growth potential than the market recognizes. Be the talent that can see beyond the present valuation to the intrinsic worth of opportunities.

The Power of Compound Interest: Buffett's wealth wasn't built overnight. Similarly, professional growth is a compound interest of skills and experiences. Focus on accumulating small, continuous improvements in your skillset and network. Over time, these will amass to a significant advantage in your career.

Risk Management through Diversification: Just as Buffett never puts all his financial eggs in one basket, diversify your professional portfolio. Develop a breadth of skills and cultivate various income streams to mitigate career risks. Like a wellbalanced portfolio, this can protect you during industry downturns and economic upheavals.

LongTerm Vision Over Immediate Gratification: Buffett is renowned for his longterm investment outlook. In your career, resist the temptation for immediate payoff in favor of longterm professional goals. Whether it's turning down a lucrative offer for a role that offers better growth potential or investing in learning a new skill that doesn't pay off immediately, prioritize your longterm career trajectory.

Financial Literacy as a Core Skill: For Buffett, understanding finances is key. Similarly, no matter your field, gain a working knowledge of financial principles. This literacy will allow you to make better decisions and communicate more effectively with the financial stakeholders in your organization.

Embrace the Circle of Competence: Buffett doesn't venture into investments he doesn't understand. Know your professional strengths and capitalize on them. Recognize the edge of your expertise and collaborate with others when venturing beyond it, leveraging collective knowledge.

Frugality as Efficiency: The billionaire's frugality is legendary. Apply this principle by optimizing resource use in your career. Make strategic decisions that require less investment—whether it's time, money, or energy—for a greater return. It's not about being cheap, but about being efficient.

The Principle of Inaction: Often, Buffett's most strategic moves are those he doesn't make. Similarly, know when not to make a career move.

Sometimes, staying put, consolidating your position, and deepening your expertise is the most strategic decision.

By integrating these principles, derived from the approach of financial maestro Warren Buffett, we can cultivate a financially savvy approach to career development.

08

Ethics in Action

In the dynamic world of business, where ambition often takes the lead, there's a more subtle, yet equally critical path: establishing ethical cornerstones. This journey isn't just about legal compliance, it's about aligning with a moral compass that steers you through both familiar and unknown challenges.

Imagine taking the reins of a company. In this role, your actions set the tone for ethical conduct, far more than any words could. This process is similar to constructing a building — the integrity of the entire structure hinges on the robustness of its foundational cornerstones. The journey of ethical leadership starts with deep self-awareness, an understanding of your own core values and beliefs. Such introspection is vital, as these principles form the base of your professional decision-making framework.

Creating a commitment to ethics in a professional landscape is an ongoing endeavor, not just a one-off declaration. Think of it as a dynamic process, where every decision and action, guided by integrity, shapes and defines your leadership identity.

Consider the development of a commitment to ethics as a process of growth and deepening understanding, much like the way a tree strengthens its roots while reaching skyward. A true commitment to ethics is about continually deepening your grasp and connection to your core values. This deepening involves persistent learning, self-reflection, and surrounding yourself with colleagues and mentors who respect and, importantly, challenge your ethical perspectives. It's about fostering an environment where ethical dialogues are welcomed and actively promoted.

Throughout this journey, it's essential to recognize that embracing an ethical code isn't about being flawless. It's about the genuine intent, consistent effort, and a deep-seated commitment to act ethically, benefiting yourself and everyone in your professional circle. It entails becoming a pillar of trust and integrity amid the ever-present uncertainties, guiding your own career trajectory and positively influencing others to raise their ethical standards.

Setting a Personal Ethical Code and Embracing Ethics at Every Level

For the ambitious professional with sights set on career peaks, the development of a personal ethical code is not just beneficial, but essential. In the high-pressure, high-stakes corporate environment, the decisions you make and the way you lead are deeply intertwined with your ethical stance. Crafting a personal ethical code requires a tailored approach, one that speaks directly to the unique challenges and scenarios of your industry and role.

Defining Your Ethical Boundaries in Concrete Terms

In Negotiations: It's crucial to delineate the boundaries of ethical flexibility. Define clearly what actions or concessions would compromise your ethical standards. This might involve setting limits on the use of privileged information, determining how far you'll go in bargaining tactics, and recognizing when competitive strategies border on unethical advantages. Such pre-set boundaries ensure you navigate negotiations with integrity.

In Leadership: Here, ethical leadership manifests in daily operational choices. This involves creating a fair and balanced workload distribution, ensuring promotions are free from biases, and maintaining a workplace environment free of harassment and discrimination. Remember, your actions and policies set the tone for ethical behavior within the team.

Cultivating Ethical Leadership Qualities

Begin by internalizing key leadership qualities seen in successful CEOs, such as foresight, responsibility, and integrity. Reflect on how these qualities can be manifested in your current role. For instance, show foresight by anticipating the long-term impacts of your actions, take responsibility for both successes and failures, and consistently act with integrity.

Implementing Ethics in Decision-Making

Ethical decision-making must be systematic and deliberate. Develop a framework that incorporates ethical considerations at every decision point. For example, when faced with cost-cutting choices, evaluate not just the financial implications but also the impact on team morale, employee well-being, and customer satisfaction. This holistic approach to decision-making ensures that ethical considerations are not an afterthought but a fundamental part of the process.

Enhancing Ethical Awareness

Regularly engage with resources that enhance your understanding of ethics in your field. This could be through professional development courses, attending industry seminars, or keeping abreast of current ethical discussions in your field. The goal is to continuously refine your understanding and application of ethics in a professional context.

Ethical Communication as a Career Tool

Honesty and transparency should be the cornerstones of your communication style. This involves openly giving credit to others, owning up to your errors, and being transparent about your motives and decisions. Whether it's providing candid feedback during reviews or openly discussing company policy changes, your communication should reflect your ethical standards.

Ethical Influence in Your Professional Sphere

Leverage your position to champion ethical behavior. Mentor emerging leaders in navigating ethical challenges, advocate for corporate policies that uphold ethical standards, and engage in community initiatives that align with your ethical values. By doing so, you are encouraging ethical behavior within your sphere of influence.

Navigating Ethical Dilemmas

Prepare a strategy for ethical dilemmas, which are inevitable as you ascend in your career. Establish clear protocols for instances such as conflicts of interest - this might involve recusing yourself from certain decisions or seeking guidance from an ethics committee. Having a plan in place ensures you handle these situations with integrity and transparency.

Adapting and Evolving Your Ethical Code

As you climb higher in your professional journey, the complexity of ethical challenges you face will likely increase. It's important to regularly revisit and update your ethical code to reflect new responsibilities, evolving societal norms, and emerging challenges in your industry.

By crafting and steadfastly adhering to a personal ethical code, you are protecting your integrity and significantly bolstering your professional reputation. This reputation for ethical leadership becomes a distinguishing factor in a competitive career landscape.

Leaders known for ethical conduct are often viewed as more reliable, trustworthy, and equipped to handle high-stakes situations. In today's world, where ethical lapses can lead to significant professional and personal consequences, your unwavering commitment to ethical practices is not merely a moral stance but a strategic tool for enduring career success and advancement.

Building on the principles of establishing a personal ethical code, I would like to relate how the same was tied into my professional journey.

This strategy evolved into a fundamental aspect of my professional philosophy, highlighting the importance of distinguishing between issues that can be resolved and situations that are irretrievable. Often, upholding ethical standards and personal well-being meant stepping back and acknowledging that letting go can be just as important as persevering.

This experience has significantly shaped my approach to leadership and the way I guide my team. I've emphasized the value of resilience, but equally, I've underscored the importance of recognizing when to withdraw from a futile endeavor for the greater benefit. It's about balancing empathy with a realistic assessment of the situation and pairing perseverance with the wisdom to know when restraint is the better part of valor.

Navigating the complexities of customer service has been instrumental in honing my problem-solving skills and molding my ethos as a leader. This journey underscores the delicate balance between empathy and practicality, and between steadfast determination and the discernment to know when to let go. It's a balance that is crucial not just in customer service, but in all facets of professional growth and ethical leadership.

Building Trust with Openness: Embracing Transparency as a Growth Tool

We have seen how building trust through transparency is not just an ethical choice but a strategic necessity. Transparency in business practices, decision-making processes, and internal communication fosters a culture of trust that is essential for long-term success. It creates an environment where employees feel valued and involved, customers feel respected and loyal, and stakeholders feel assured and committed.

A prime example of how ethical leadership and transparency can drive growth is The Tata Group, one of India's largest and oldest conglomerates. The group's journey offers valuable insights into how ethical principles can be woven into a company's culture and operations.

How Tata's Ethical Stance Inspires Professional Growth

Foundational Ethical Practices

At the core of Tata's philosophy is a commitment to ethics and integrity, evident in their business operations, social responsibilities, and corporate governance. Tata has institutionalized ethics through mechanisms like Tata Business Excellence Model (TBEM) and Tata Code of Conduct (TCoC), ensuring that ethical practices are not just aspirational but actionable.

Employee Engagement and Development

Tata places a high emphasis on employee engagement and development. This approach includes robust training programs, transparent promotion practices, and avenues for employees to provide feedback on company policies. Such practices enhance job satisfaction and encourage employees to align their personal growth with the company's ethical standards.

Innovation Within Ethical Boundaries

The group encourages innovation within the framework of ethical practices. This unique approach has led to groundbreaking products and services that adhere to sustainability and social responsibility, inspiring employees to think creatively while staying grounded in ethical values.

Brand Trust and Global Recognition

Tata's unwavering commitment to ethics has built a brand trusted globally, attracting top talent and opening doors to international markets. Employees associated with Tata often find that their career prospects are enhanced by the group's reputation for integrity and social responsibility.

Leadership and Ethical Advocacy

The group's leadership is actively involved in advocating for ethical practices in the business community. This advocacy extends beyond the company, influencing policies and practices in the wider corporate world, thus shaping a more ethical business landscape.

The Tata Group's approach to ethical leadership and transparency demonstrates how these practices can be powerful catalysts for both organizational and individual growth. For professionals seeking career advancement, this underscores the importance of aligning personal values with business practices and the potential of ethical leadership to create not just successful but also sustainable career paths. In the modern business world, transparency and ethics are not just moral imperatives, they are strategic tools for building a resilient, trusted, and forward-thinking professional identity.

09

Worldview: Embracing Global Perspectives

Picture yourself, a young professional, stepping into a multinational corporation. You're surrounded by colleagues from various cultural backgrounds, each bringing a unique set of experiences and viewpoints. Here, the workplace becomes a melting pot of ideas, perspectives, and approaches. Embracing this diversity is about actively engaging and learning from these myriad perspectives to propel your career forward.

When you are in a team where everyone comes from similar backgrounds and experiences, the problem-solving approach tends to be linear and uniform. Now, contrast this with a diverse team. Here, each member, influenced by their cultural context, approaches problems from different angles. In my previous role, I faced an intriguing challenge - stepping into a role where my mission was to ignite rapid growth in an industry as intricate and regulated as pharmaceuticals. I was spearheading an internal startup-like initiative aimed at shattering traditional growth ceilings. But the approach we took was anything but conventional.

Instead of assembling a team solely from pharmaceutical veterans, we cast a wider net, seeking out professionals with diverse backgrounds and fresh perspectives. Our leadership team became a culmination of varied experiences: an ex-entrepreneur who was a Non-Resident Indian (NRI) from the Middle East, known for his innovative thinking and global business acumen; a supply chain specialist whose insights were honed by years of managing complex operations; and a finance expert with a keen eye for sustainable growth strategies. None had direct pharmaceutical industry experience, but all brought something more valuable: a shared sense of curiosity, a 'how not to' mindset challenging industry norms, and a relentless spirit to innovate and excel.

This deliberate blend of diverse backgrounds and perspectives created a vibrant environment where traditional approaches were deconstructed, and innovative strategies emerged. Our meetings became melting pots of ideas, where the entrepreneurial spirit of the NRI clashed and then melded with the methodical precision of the supply chain and finance experts. Each discussion, each strategy session was a journey through different cultural and professional landscapes, offering fresh insights and unconventional solutions.

The impact was profound. In just six months, this diverse team defied industry standards by developing a business model that not only grew by over 30X but also established a solid foundational process that promised continued growth and innovation. This wasn't just growth, it was transformation, driven by a team whose diverse experiences became our strongest asset.

This experience became a defining moment in my career, reinforcing my belief that while industry expertise is invaluable, it is the diversity of thought and experience that truly ignites transformative success. It's a lesson in the power of diversity, not just in culture but in professional background and thinking. In the world of business, particularly in fields as complex as pharmaceuticals, it's this diversity that drives innovation, excellence, and, ultimately, unprecedented growth.

The Diversity Synergy Matrix

Reflecting on this successful integration of diverse perspectives, which significantly boosted innovation and growth, we can further explore the structured application of such diversity in career development. This brings us to the Diversity Synergy Matrix. The matrix is a multifaceted approach designed to harness cultural diversity for career growth. It incorporates a series of interconnected strategies, each a critical component in building a solid, diversity-driven career path.

The Empathy Strategy

Beyond the basics of listening, this strategy involves interpreting the underlying cultural nuances in communication. For instance, understanding high-context communication styles, prevalent in many Asian cultures, where not everything is verbalized explicitly. Developing this skill can lead to better collaboration and less misunderstanding in multicultural teams. It's about listening to what is said, how it's said, and what might not be said aloud but is still communicated.

The Collaboration Strategy

This strategy is more than just gathering diverse opinions; it's about creating an environment where every member feels their input is valued and considered. This might involve structuring meetings to allow for anonymous idea submission or using digital platforms that enable equal participation from all team members, regardless of their location or time zone. Such inclusivity not only democratizes the idea generation process but also encourages a wider range of innovative solutions.

The Synergy Strategy

In implementing this strategy, it's essential to recognize and utilize the strengths that different cultural perspectives bring to a project. For example, combining the holistic, big-picture approach often found in Western cultures with the meticulous, detail-oriented approach prevalent in East Asian cultures can lead to more comprehensive project outcomes. It's about creating a synergy where the sum of collaborative efforts is greater than individual contributions.

The Insight Strategy

Engaging in cultural sensitivity training should go beyond generic programs. Tailored training that addresses specific cultural dynamics relevant to your industry or team composition is more effective. This could include scenario-based learning to navigate cultural differences in real-world business situations, enhancing your ability to interact respectfully and effectively with colleagues from diverse backgrounds.

The Guidance Strategy

Building a diverse mentorship network involves actively seeking mentors who can offer different perspectives based on their cultural backgrounds and experiences. This network should be a mix of senior leaders, peers from different departments or industries, and even junior staff who can provide fresh, grassroots-level insights. Such a diversified mentorship approach ensures a well-rounded professional development.

The Benchmarking Strategy

This strategy involves studying global best practices and critically analyzing how they can be adapted or improved in your specific context. For instance, if you're in marketing, understanding how brands successfully navigate cultural nuances in different regions can offer valuable lessons. The key is to not just emulate but to innovate based on these learnings.

The Learning Strategy

Deep diving into case studies of diverse teams, this strategy focuses on understanding the dynamics that led to their success or failure. Analyzing cases where cultural diversity played a key role in problem-solving or innovation can provide actionable insights on managing diversity effectively. This should include a critical review of both successful and unsuccessful team endeavors, learning from the challenges as much as the triumphs.

The Foundation Strategy

Advocating for diverse hiring practices entails actively participating in or influencing the recruitment process to ensure a wide range of candidates are considered. This involves looking beyond traditional recruitment methods to tap into diverse talent pools, working with HR to eliminate biases in job descriptions, and ensuring that interview panels are diverse themselves, to minimize unconscious bias.

Each of these strategies within the Diversity Synergy Matrix Framework offers a detailed, actionable approach to leveraging cultural diversity for career advancement. By integrating these strategies, professionals can cultivate a more inclusive, innovative, and globally-minded approach to their career development, positioning themselves for success in an increasingly interconnected world.

Individual Adaptation of Global Strategies for Local Relevance

Embracing global strategies and tailoring them to fit the local context is a transformative personal journey, one that I've navigated through firsthand at Kaay Innovation.

In the landscape of SaaS, where every solution claims to be the next big thing, we at Kaay Innovation faced a unique challenge. Our mission was clear: develop SaaS products that not only met international standards but also resonated deeply with the Indian market. This task entailed understanding and connecting with a diverse and vibrant culture.

As we embarked on this journey, we realized that localization involves much more than translating content. It's about understanding the subtle cultural preferences that can make or break user engagement. For instance, while our global counterparts leaned towards minimalistic designs and self-service platforms, our Indian users preferred a different approach. They were drawn to platforms that felt familiar and intuitive, with vibrant color schemes, larger fonts, and more guided experiences. This became a revelation about how deeply cultural nuances are woven into the fabric of user preferences.

We didn't stop at aesthetic adjustments. Incorporating blogs and communities into our SaaS offerings, a trend globally, needed a local twist. For our B2B sector, the content needed to be more than just informative; it had to offer tangible value for their businesses. Meanwhile, for our B2C audience, we spiced up the content to be more entertainment-oriented, creating an engaging and relatable user experience.

This journey wasn't a solitary one. It was a collaborative effort filled with conversations, feedback, and a shared vision of creating something truly impactful. The result was nothing short of remarkable. Within just six months, we witnessed our business grow exponentially, revealing the power of precise, culturally attuned adaptation.

As we move to the next section, I want to shift the focus from what we achieved at Kaay Innovation to how you, as an individual, can embrace and apply these strategies in your professional journey. Adapting global strategies to local contexts goes beyond business models and product features; it's about a mindset, a way of seeing and understanding the world that can significantly enhance your professional path.

So, as we delve deeper, remember: the journey of adapting global strategies is as much about understanding others as it is about understanding yourself. It's about finding that sweet spot where your skills, insights, and innovations meet the unique needs and nuances of the local market.

Gathering Contextual Intelligence: Your Pathway to Market Insight

Understanding your market goes beyond the surface. Dive deep into the cultural nuances, consumer behavior, and economic conditions that define your local environment. Attend local events, engage in online forums specific to the region, or conduct your surveys. Professionals can utilize tools like Google Trends to understand local market interests or platforms like SurveyMonkey for targeted market surveys to gather deep insights.

This hands-on approach makes you a go-to resource in your organization, someone known for having their finger on the pulse of the market.

Engaging with Local Stakeholders: Building Bridges and Brands

Engaging with local stakeholders transforms a routine task into an opportunity for personal growth. Forge genuine relationships with customers, partners, and even competitors. Each interaction is a chance to build your personal brand as a culturally savvy and globally competent professional. Volunteer for local projects, seek mentorship, or lead community initiatives. Each step you take shapes your personal narrative within the local business culture. Let's take the instance of sales here. In sales, building trust is crucial. Sales professionals can organize community events or workshops to engage directly with their local customers, similar to how a major brand might run a focus group to understand consumer needs better. This direct engagement is invaluable for tailoring pitches and products to local tastes.

Tailoring Products and Services: Your Innovation Showcase

Suggesting adjustments or introducing new features that reflect local tastes does more than boost sales. It spotlights your capacity for innovative thinking and problem-solving. It's about seeing through the customer's eyes and anticipating their needs even before they do. This proactive stance on customization marks you as a forward-thinking asset to any team. If you are in marketing, you can use A/B testing to see which product features or advertisements resonate more with the local audience.You can then use this data to inform decisions, ensuring that the offerings are perfectly tuned to local preferences.

Adapting Communication: Cultivating Influence and Understanding

Mastering the art of communication in diverse settings is pivotal. Whether it's picking up key phrases in another language or understanding the subtleties of non-verbal cues, each effort you make enhances your effectiveness and expands your influence. It's about connecting, understanding, and being understood—a triad that powers successful careers. For instance, if you are a project manager working with a diverse team, you mightt use tools like Slack or Trello, which support various languages and time zones, to ensure clear, inclusive communication. You can also also take short courses on cultural communication to enhance their interaction with team members from different backgrounds.

Fostering Diverse Teams and Partnerships: Expanding Your Professional Ecosystem

Championing diversity in your team or forging local partnerships isn't just about broadening your professional network; it's about enriching your perspective. Diverse teams challenge you to think differently, approach problems creatively, and discover innovative solutions. Each partnership brings new opportunities for learning and growth, setting you up as a professional who thrives on collaboration and diversity.

Embracing Continuous Feedback: Showcasing Your Adaptability

Integrating feedback into your work rhythm showcases your commitment to continuous improvement. Whether it's customer reviews, peer evaluations, or self-reflection, each piece of feedback is a stepping stone to better performance and higher career altitudes. It reflects an adaptable, responsive professional ethos, qualities that are gold in today's dynamic work environments.

Staying Informed on Local Competitors: Keeping Your Edge

Keeping an eye on local competitors is more than market research; it's about staying ahead. Understand their strategies, learn from their successes and failures, and use this knowledge to anticipate market shifts. This proactive approach ensures you're always a step ahead, ready with solutions and suggestions that keep your organization at the forefront.

Upholding Compliance and Ethics: Cultivating Trust and Integrity

A solid understanding and adherence to local laws and ethical standards solidify your reputation as a reliable and trustworthy professional. It's a commitment that speaks volumes about your character and professional integrity, traits that underpin successful, long-lasting careers.

By incorporating these strategies into your professional life, you position yourself as an indispensable asset to your organization. You become the professional who not only understands the global vision but also translates it into local success. This approach sets a new standard for what it means to be a globally-minded, locally-attuned professional.

IKEA in India: A Case Study on Global Strategy Adaptation for Professional Insights

IKEA, the world's largest furniture retailer, headquartered in the Netherlands and founded in Sweden 77 years ago, is celebrated for its affordable, trendy, and ready-to-assemble furniture. Its recent venture into India, a market known for its young and aspirational population, is a striking example of successful global strategy adaptation, offering valuable lessons for professionals striving for career ascension.

IKEA's Glocalization Strategy in India

Strategic Store Locations

IKEA's decision to open its first store in Hyderabad, an IT hub with a young and urban population, reflects a deep understanding of the local demographic. The store's overwhelming footfall of over 4 million visitors since its inauguration in August 2018 set the stage for further expansion into Mumbai, Bengaluru, and Gurgaon—cities chosen for their similar demographic profiles. This decision-making process underscores the importance of market research and demographic alignment in global strategy adaptation.

Customization in Furniture Assembly

Recognizing the Indian market's unfamiliarity with self-assembly furniture, IKEA partnered with Urban Company, facilitating furniture assembly services for customers. This strategic move to align with the Indian mindset and habits illustrates the importance of understanding and adapting to local consumer behaviors.

Innovative Delivery Solutions

Utilizing solar-powered auto-rickshaws for deliveries, IKEA aligned itself culturally and environmentally with the local context. This innovative approach enhanced brand association with a familiar Indian symbol and reflected IKEA's commitment to sustainability, addressing India's air pollution concerns.

Localized Product and Pricing Strategy

Adapting its product range, IKEA localized over 1,000 products, catering to Indian materials and sourcing preferences. Additionally, IKEA's introduction of a lower-priced product section acknowledges the price sensitivity of the Indian market. This approach exemplifies the importance of product and pricing strategies that resonate with local market conditions.

Professional Insights from IKEA's India Strategy

Market Research and Demographic Alignment

Professionals can learn the value of in-depth market research and choosing locations or markets that align with their business offerings. Understanding the local demographic is key to positioning oneself or one's products effectively.

Adaptation to Local Consumer Behaviors

IKEA's strategy demonstrates the importance of aligning with local consumer habits and preferences. Professionals should consider local customs, habits, and preferences in their strategies to ensure better acceptance and success.

Innovation in Response to Local Needs

IKEA's use of solar-powered auto-rickshaws represents a blend of cultural understanding and innovative problem-solving. Professionals should strive to find creative solutions that address local needs while also aligning with broader organizational goals.

Product Localization and Sensitivity to Pricing

Adapting products to local tastes and being sensitive to pricing strategies are crucial in different markets. Professionals should consider how they can tailor their offerings to meet the unique needs and economic realities of each market they serve.

IKEA's successful entry and planned expansion in India, aiming to open 25 stores by 2025, demonstrate the effectiveness of its market entry strategy. For professionals, this case study serves as an exemplary model of adapting global strategies to local contexts, highlighting the importance of cultural sensitivity, market research, innovation, and adaptation in achieving career growth and success in global markets.

Unifying Diverse Teams: Adopting a CEO's Strategy to Align Varied Backgrounds

Building on the insights from IKEA's successful adaptation of global strategies to the Indian market, let's shift focus to the individual professional level, specifically on understanding how a global perspective enhances career trajectories.

Let's explore how the principles of unifying diverse teams, balancing global ambitions with local connections, and cultivating a global perspective can drive career growth.

Empathy as a Leadership Skill

Deep Active Listening: This entails understanding the context, the emotions, and the unspoken nuances in communication. Empathetic leaders can decode the underlying concerns or aspirations of their team members.

Cultural Sensitivity: Empathy in a diverse team setting requires sensitivity to cultural differences. This means understanding and respecting varied communication styles, decision-making processes, and work ethics influenced by cultural backgrounds.

Personalizing Management Approaches: Recognize that one size does not fit all in team management. Empathetic leaders tailor their approach to suit the individual needs and strengths of team members, which can significantly boost morale and productivity.

Building Trust and Respect

Consistency and Integrity: Trust is built through consistent actions and decision-making that upholds integrity. This means making commitments carefully and following through on them.

Open and Transparent Communication: Foster an environment where team members feel comfortable voicing their ideas and concerns without fear of judgment or retribution.

Empowerment and Autonomy: Demonstrate trust in team members' abilities by giving them autonomy and the space to take initiative. This builds respect and encourages a sense of ownership and responsibility among team members.

Vision and Goal Alignment

Crafting a Compelling Narrative

Inclusive Storytelling: Create a vision narrative that includes diverse perspectives and reflects the collective aspirations of the team. This could involve co-creating the vision with team input, making it more inclusive and representative.

Connecting Individual Goals to the Larger Vision: Demonstrate how each team member's role and personal goals contribute to the broader organizational objectives. This alignment helps in creating a more engaged and motivated team.

Shared Objectives

Collaborative Goal Setting: Involve team members in the goal-setting process, this ensures that the objectives are collectively owned and more meaningful to everyone.

Celebrating Diverse Contributions: Acknowledge and celebrate the unique contributions each team member brings to achieving shared goals. This recognition fosters a sense of belonging and validates the importance of diverse skills and perspectives.

Cultural Competence

Inclusive Leadership

Active Integration of Diverse Perspectives: This involves listening to diverse viewpoints , actively seeking them out and integrating them into decision-making and strategy formulation. It requires a conscious effort to ensure that all voices, especially those that are typically underrepresented, are heard and valued.

Decision-Making Inclusivity: Implement decision-making processes that reflect a range of cultural perspectives. This could mean incorporating collaborative decision-making styles or consensus-building approaches that are more inclusive.

Celebrating Diversity

Cultural Learning and Sharing: Organizing events or initiatives where team members can share their cultural backgrounds and learn from each other. This could range from cultural presentations to celebrating a wide array of cultural festivities in the workplace.

Diversity as a Source of Innovation: Recognize and leverage the diverse cultural backgrounds of team members as a source of creative ideas and solutions. Encouraging teams to view diversity as a strength that can lead to more innovative and effective problem-solving.

Adapting to Local and Global Markets

Understanding Local Markets

Deep Market Analysis: Gobeyond surface-level understandings to analyze local consumer needs, preferences, and behaviors using data analytics, local market surveys, and other research tools.

Cultural Sensitivity in Marketing: Craft marketing campaigns that are not only translated but culturally adapted, ensuring they resonate with local audiences.

Customizing Strategies

Flexibility in Implementation: Adapt global strategies with enough flexibility to allow for local customization. This could mean altering product features, marketing strategies, or even business models to better suit local markets.

Local Innovations for Global Application: Recognize successful local strategies or products that have the potential to be scaled globally.

Cultivating Global and Local Networks

Strategic Networking

Purpose-Driven Networking: Actively seek connections that align with specific business goals, whether it's finding local partners, understanding local market dynamics, or identifying global trends.

Diverse Network Building: Ensure that the professional network is diverse in terms of geography, industry, and cultural background, which broadens the range of insights and opportunities available.

Leveraging Local Insights for Global Success

Feedback Loops: Establish mechanisms to regularly gather and analyze local insights, ensuring these insights inform and improve global strategies.

Local Success Stories: Identify and learn from local success stories, which can provide valuable lessons for global strategy development.

Enhancing Career Trajectories with a Global Perspective

Expanding Career Opportunities

Career Mobility

International Exposure: This entails seeking roles and projects that offer international exposure, either through physical relocation or virtual teams, to understand and engage with global markets.

Language and Cultural Learning: Investing in language skills and cultural learning to enhance communication and understanding in international settings.

Cross-Cultural Collaboration

Interdisciplinary Teams: Working in or leading teams composed of members from various cultural and professional backgrounds to gain experience in navigating and leveraging cross-cultural dynamics.

Conflict Resolution in Diverse Settings: Developing skills in managing and resolving conflicts that may arise from cultural misunderstandings or differing viewpoints.

Developing a Global Mindset

Innovative Problem-Solving

Exposure to Varied Business Practices: Seeking opportunities to learn about different business practices and models from around the world, either through formal education, professional experiences, or personal research.

Creative Application of Global Insights: Applying insights gained from global exposure to bring innovative solutions to local or organizational challenges.

Adaptability and Resilience

Cultivating Flexibility: Actively developing the ability to adapt to new environments, work cultures, and business practices.

Building Resilience: Learning to navigate and thrive amidst the uncertainties and challenges that come with operating in a global environment, which can be crucial for long-term career success and satisfaction.

These strategies encompass a holistic approach to leveraging cultural competence, balancing global and local market dynamics, and developing a global mindset.

10

Turning Points and Graceful Transitions

Mastering career transitions is crucial in the journey of professional growth. These moments, whether it's about switching roles, diving into a new industry, or choosing to hit the pause button, are more than just career milestones. They shape your professional story in ways that are often profound and far-reaching.

Let's talk about timing. It's all about knowing when to make your move. This isn't just about keeping an eye on market trends or job openings, it's as much about tuning in to your own career aspirations and readiness. Knowing when to leap into a new challenge or when to take a step back for some growth and reflection can really set you apart in your career journey.

I would like to relate the story of Kavya, a peer from B-school who climbed her way up to become a standout marketing executive in a top tech company. Kavya had this knack for being ahead of the curve. When she saw the wave of AI-driven marketing coming, she didn't just watch from the sidelines. She dived into learning about AI and brought this new skill set into her marketing role. It was more than just a career shift; it was a strategic move that really put her in the spotlight of industry innovation.

Then there's Aarav, someone I worked with early in my career. He was the kind of guy who seemed to be on the fast track to success. But even the fastest engines need a cool-down. When he started feeling burned out, he didn't just push through. He pressed pause and took a sabbatical to rethink and realign his goals. This break wasn't a setback. In fact, it was the opposite. Aarav came back recharged and eventually started his own successful consulting business.

The experiences of Kavya and Aarav teach us a valuable lesson about the timing of career transitions. It's about being smart with your choices – knowing when to jump on an opportunity and when to take a break for self-development. These decisions are crucial in treading through your career path with grace and success.

Navigating these transitions is a major driver of your professional development. It's about making choices that align with both your personal goals and the evolving job landscape. Done right, these moves can open up exciting new paths.

Desire and Deserving: The 2Ds of Career Progression

During my second year in my second job, I encountered a moment of profound revelation about career ascension. It happened during an appraisal session, a meeting that I anticipated with a mix of excitement and nervous energy. Recognized as a high performer and known for my zeal, I had high hopes for this discussion with senior management. My regular visits to the regional office were always energizing, and the buzz about this particular meeting, rumored to be about a potential promotion, added an extra layer of anticipation.

As the meeting unfolded, led by a senior colleague known for his punctuality and discipline (traits I admired and emulated), the conversation naturally veered toward my future in the company. When prompted about my career ambitions, I didn't hesitate. I expressed my strong desire for a promotion, ready and eager to shoulder greater responsibilities and undertake more challenging assignments. However, his response took me by surprise and led to a significant shift in my thinking. He posed a simple yet profound question: "Do you Deserve or Desire?"

This question made me pause and reflect deeply. It highlighted the nuanced difference between 'Desire' and 'Deserving'. While I had clearly articulated my desires, he pointed out the crucial importance of 'Deserving'. This concept extends beyond ambition. He elaborated that truly deserving candidates are those who already function at the level they aspire to reach, effectively sidestepping the pitfalls described in 'the Peter Principle', where individuals ascend to levels of incompetence.

This conversation marked a definitive moment in my career trajectory. It led me to adopt a more balanced approach – one that harmonizes aspiration with concrete action. In navigating career transitions, whether shifting roles or moving within an organization, it became clear that embodying the role you aspire to is essential. It's about ensuring that your actions, your contributions, and your work ethic reflect the position you aim to hold.

The idea is to be someone who doesn't just aim for the next level but behaves as if they have already reached it. This proactive and forward-thinking approach positions you not merely as a candidate who desires a new role but as one who truly deserves it. It's about demonstrating through your actions and results that you are not just ready but are effectively operating at that next level. This philosophy turns aspirations into realities and transforms the journey of career advancement into a pathway marked by deserved achievements and meaningful progress.

Howard Schultz's Starbucks Stint: A Reflection of Personal Growth and Organizational Influence

Howard Schultz's tenure at Starbucks stands as a remarkable illustration of how individual evolution can powerfully impact and transform a corporation. His journey with Starbucks is not just a tale of business acumen; it is a nuanced portrayal of how personal development intricately weaves into the fabric of career ascension and organizational influence.

Starbucks Before Schultz's Reinvention

Initially, Starbucks, a modest coffee bean retailer, had not yet realized its potential for a broader cultural impact. This phase in Starbucks' history is similar to the early stages of a professional career where potential is abundant but not yet fully realized or harnessed. It's a stage where foundational skills are developed, much like the initial steps in the FRAME method, laying the groundwork for future growth.

Schultz's Personal Growth Journey Reflected in Starbucks

When Schultz joined Starbucks, he brought with him not just ambition but a vision fostered by his personal experiences and insights – a testament to the importance of continuous learning and adaptability in career ascension. His inspiration from Italian espresso bars and his vision for Starbucks as a 'third place' for community highlights the importance of innovative thinking and the willingness to embrace new ideas, resonating with the strategies discussed earlier for managing professional fatigue.

Schultz's initial struggle to pivot Starbucks' business model mirrors the challenges faced in making strategic career transitions. His resilience in this period, choosing to start Il Giornale after facing resistance, reflects the earlier discussions about discerning when to pivot or pause in one's career. This move was a strategic risk, showcasing the necessity of courage and foresight in career ascension.

His return to Starbucks and the subsequent transformation of the company underscore how a leader's personal growth can be a driving force for organizational change. Schultz's focus on creating a culture that valued and cared for its employees aligns with the principles of the FRAME method and fostering a supportive work environment. His approach to rapid expansion, and later, the recognition of overexpansion, demonstrates the application of self-awareness and strategic adaptation in a professional context.

Under Schultz, Starbucks' evolution was not just about business strategies but also about nurturing a culture of belonging and community. Schultz's emphasis on culture, community, and employee well-being was instrumental in redefining the Starbucks experience, aligning perfectly with the principles of sustaining high performance through personal well-being and work-life balance.

Schultz's journey with Starbucks vividly illustrates how personal development, strategic thinking, and resilience are essential in advancing one's career and in spearheading significant organizational change. His story resonates deeply, serving as a reminder that professional success is deeply linked to personal growth and the capacity to inspire transformative changes.

11

Recharge and Resolve

In the relentless pursuit of professional success, emotional wellness often takes a backseat, overshadowed by immediate targets and tangible achievements. However, neglecting this aspect can lead to burnout, decreased productivity, and ultimately, a decline in performance. The key to sustained success lies not just in skill and determination but also in maintaining a healthy emotional state.

Emotional wellness in the workplace is multifaceted. It encompasses the ability to manage stress effectively, maintain a positive work-life balance, and cultivate a supportive work environment. Research in organizational psychology consistently highlights the correlation between emotional well-being and professional effectiveness. Employees who report higher levels of emotional wellness tend to exhibit greater creativity, better problem-solving abilities, and improved decision-making skills.

One essential aspect of fostering emotional wellness is stress management. The modern workplace is often a hub of high pressure and tight deadlines, making stress an inevitable part of professional life. However, the manner in which we handle this stress can profoundly impact our overall performance. Techniques such as mindfulness, meditation, and regular physical exercise have been shown to significantly reduce stress levels. Companies are increasingly recognizing the importance of these practices, incorporating wellness programs into their employee benefits.

Another critical component is the cultivation of a positive work-life balance. This balance is not about an equal division of hours between work and personal life, but rather about achieving a harmony that optimizes both personal well-being and professional productivity. Flexible work arrangements, regular breaks, and time for personal pursuits are essential in maintaining this balance.

The role of the work environment in emotional wellness cannot be overstated. A supportive and inclusive workplace culture, where open communication and mutual respect are the norms, contributes significantly to the emotional health of employees. Leaders play a crucial role in shaping this culture, modeling empathy, and understanding, and fostering an environment where feedback is constructive, and failures are viewed as learning opportunities.

Work & Life + 1: The FRAME Method for Work-Life Balance

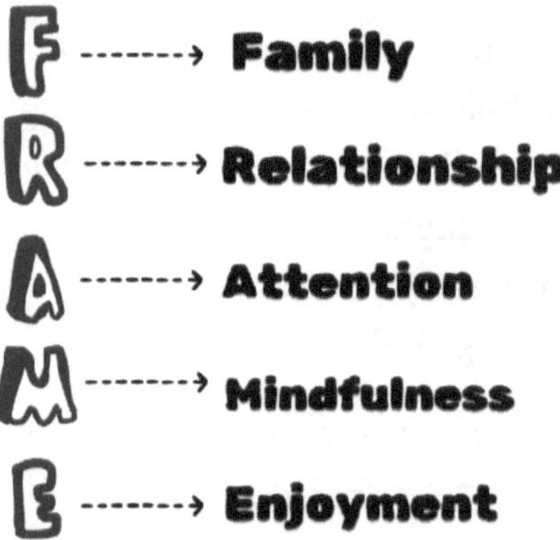

In the continuous journey of balancing professional commitments with personal life, many individuals struggle to find harmony, even when they have sufficient leisure time. This struggle often culminates in moments of reflection, perhaps on a Sunday evening, pondering over the thought, "Could I have utilized my weekend more effectively?" This is a common sentiment, echoing the experiences of many professionals who find striking the right balance challenging.

One of the most profound lessons I learned came from an unexpected source - a monk I encountered during a trip to Bhutan in 2015. His words, "Earn to live, not live to earn," resonated deeply with me. This wisdom doesn't imply that one should not be ambitious or work hard. Instead, it suggests that our professional endeavors should bring a sense of peace and fulfillment, not just financial rewards and exhaustion.

To embody this philosophy, I adopted the 5-step FRAME method, a transformative approach to achieving a more balanced life:

Family: The first step is aligning your family with your work and aspirations. It's about making a conscious effort to spend quality time with them, transcending beyond passive activities like watching movies. For older family members, this could involve offering more substantial support and assistance. It's about creating moments that are enriching and valuable for everyone involved.

Relationship: This step focuses on the intersection of your work-life balance and your home life. It involves setting up a schedule that honors your professional responsibilities while also nurturing your personal relationships. The key is to avoid letting work intrude constantly into home life, like constantly checking office emails or calls, which can strain relationships.

Attention: Paying undivided attention to the task or person at hand is crucial, whether at work or with family. Avoid multitasking and practice the art of being fully present. This focused attention enhances the quality of your interactions and productivity, making each moment count.

Mindfulness: Being mindful means being fully aware of your thoughts and emotions without being overwhelmed by them. It's about practicing mindfulness techniques to maintain a balanced and calm state of mind. This practice aids in making thoughtful decisions, contributing positively to both personal and professional spheres.

Enjoyment: Lastly, it's vital to find joy in both work and personal life. Engage in activities that are fulfilling and bring happiness. It could be anything from watching a favorite show on Netflix to browsing Instagram. The idea is to indulge in activities that you enjoy without feeling guilty or comparing your leisure choices with others.

Implementing the FRAME method is about cultivating a life that is rich in every aspect. By embracing this approach, you can create a fulfilling balance that enhances your career and enriches your personal life, leading to overall happiness and contentment.

Anticipating and Overcoming Professional Fatigue: Strategies Inspired by Top Leaders

After embracing the FRAME method for achieving work-life balance, we encounter another critical dimension in professional development: managing professional fatigue. More often a mental battle than a physical one, professional fatigue can significantly impede productivity and job satisfaction. To effectively combat this, we can look to strategies employed by top leaders who have excelled in sustaining high performance without falling prey to burnout.

Deep Dive into Understanding Professional Fatigue

Professional fatigue arises from extended periods of workplace stress and exertion. It's not just about feeling physically tired; it's a state where your motivation and engagement start to wane. Early signs, like continuous exhaustion, irritability, or a noticeable dip in the quality of work, are key indicators that should not be ignored. Recognizing these symptoms early on is crucial in proactively managing and overcoming this form of fatigue.

Learning from the Strategies of Top Leaders

Strategic Delegation: Emulating leaders like Indra Nooyi, the former CEO of PepsiCo, we find the art of delegation to be pivotal. Successful leaders understand that they don't need to shoulder every responsibility. By delegating tasks effectively to competent team members, they free up their mental space and time, focusing on broader strategic planning and critical decision-making. This practice not only reduces their workload but also empowers their teams, creating a more dynamic and proactive work environment.

Regular Detachment: The practice of detaching from work, advocated by figures like Bill Gates and Arianna Huffington, is essential for mental rejuvenation. This detachment could take various forms: from scheduling regular vacations to practicing digital detoxes during weekends, or simply carving out daily non-work time. These periods of detachment are crucial for mental recovery and maintaining a fresh perspective on work.

Mindfulness and Meditation: The incorporation of mindfulness and meditation into daily routines, as practiced by leaders like Jeff Weiner of LinkedIn, has proven benefits. These practices are not just about reducing stress; they're about cultivating a state of mental clarity. This clarity enhances decision-making, improves focus, and fosters a calm, composed approach to professional challenges.

Embracing Physical Wellness: Understanding the connection between physical and mental well-being is vital. Leaders like Barack Obama and Mark Zuckerberg prioritize regular exercise, recognizing its role in sustaining mental sharpness and resilience. Physical wellness is a cornerstone that supports mental agility and endurance, particularly crucial in high-stress professional environments.

Cultivating a Supportive Work Culture: Finally, the importance of creating and maintaining a supportive work environment, as emphasized by leaders like Sheryl Sandberg, cannot be overstated.

A culture where open communication about stress, workload, and professional challenges is encouraged goes a long way in mitigating professional fatigue. It fosters a sense of community and support, crucial for maintaining motivation and engagement.

Implementing These Strategies for Long-term Success

Adopting these strategies involves more than just occasional practice; it requires a commitment to fundamentally reshaping one's professional lifestyle. It's about recognizing the importance of your mental well-being and its direct impact on your effectiveness in your career. By incorporating these practices consistently, professionals can not only manage professional fatigue but also enhance their overall performance, ensuring longevity and satisfaction in their careers.

This comprehensive approach to combating professional fatigue, inspired by the wisdom and habits of top leaders, is about creating a lifestyle that supports enduring high performance. It underscores the importance of mental health and well-being in the professional sphere, encouraging a balanced and sustainable approach to career development.

Conclusion

As we approach the end of this journey, take a moment to reflect on the path we've walked together. From the initial steps of setting clear goals to the nuanced art of navigating career transitions, you've engaged with a spectrum of ideas and strategies.

The essence of this journey lies in the continuous pursuit of excellence. Whether it's about leading with empathy, communicating with clarity, or adapting with agility, the core message is about evolving and transcending your current self. It's about the relentless pursuit of a better you, in your career and beyond.

Remember, the potential for transformation and success lies within you. You are the architect of your destiny, capable of crafting a future as remarkable as the visions you dare to dream. As you stand at this juncture, ready to step forward, carry with you the knowledge and insights you've gained.

Now, the imperative of action calls. Understanding these principles is one thing; applying them is another. I urge you to take these insights and strategies and bring them to life in your world. Let them not just be words on a page but tools in your hands, shaping your reality.

Embrace a mindset of perpetual curiosity and determination. As T.S. Eliot beautifully put it, *"Only those who will risk going too far can possibly find out how far one can go."* Let this be your mantra. Dare to go far, pushing the boundaries of what you believe is possible.

9 798893 226652